PAPER-WEIGHTS

PAPER-WEIGHTS

THE COLLECTOR'S GUIDE TO IDENTIFYING, SELECTING, AND ENJOYING NEW AND VINTAGE PAPERWEIGHTS

Pat Reilly

KNICKERBOCKER
PRESS

Published by Knickerbocker Press
276 Fifth Avenue
New York, New York 10001

This edition produced for sale in the U.S.A., its
territories and dependencies only.

ISBN 1-57715-075-9
This edition printed 1999

A QUINTET BOOK

This book was designed and produced by
Quintet Publishing Limited
6 Blundell Street
London N7 9BH

Creative Director: Richard Dewing
Designer: Peter Laws
Project Editor: Stephanie Foster
Photographer: Martin Norris

Typeset in Great Britain by
Central Southern Typesetters, Eastbourne
Manufactured in Singapore by
Bright Arts Pte Limited
Printed in Singapore by
Star Standard Industried Pte Limited

CONTENTS

INTRODUCTION **6**

A BRIEF HISTORY OF PAPERWEIGHTS **10**

TYPES OF PAPERWEIGHT **19**

IDENTIFYING PAPERWEIGHTS **61**

GUIDE TO COLLECTING **65**

GLOSSARY **76**

PAPERWEIGHT MAKERS **77**

FURTHER READING **78**

USEFUL ADDRESSES **79**

INDEX **80**

INTRODUCTION

Functionally, a paperweight must be made of a solid material and be sufficiently compact and heavy to hold down paper. For the collector, however, it is inevitably made of glass.

It is sometimes suggested that glass paperweights have been around as long as paper, but although some of the techniques involved in their manufacture date back to glassmaking in Mesopotamia as early as the 15th century B.C., paperweights first emerged in the early 1840s, when letter writing was popular with the middle classes, and a market developed for a range of articles for the desk. In keeping with Victorian tastes, these articles were valued more for their decorative qualities than their practical application, and it is doubtful whether they were ever intended primarily to hold down paper.

ABOVE
This brightly colored, stylized bouquet from Perthshire Paperweights, made in 1986, was inspired by a well-known 19th-century St. Louis bouquet. Apart from the two flowers with the yellow match-head centers, however, the execution is all Perthshire.

BELOW
According to Baccarat, the inspiration for its 19th-century animal silhouette canes came from the animal cut-outs that the nine-year-old nephew of M. Gridel, then manager, played with. Each of

Baccarat's 20th-century Gridel series of weights reproduces all 16 of the former silhouettes of animals and birds, a man with a gun, and a red devil. The latter is the central feature of this 1977 example.

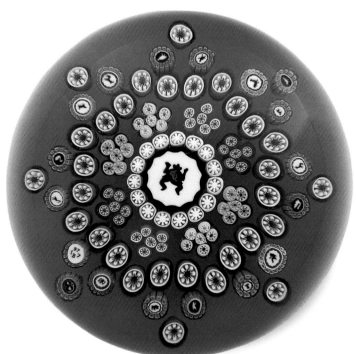

Red and white flower

Wallflower

Double clematis

Blue primrose

These four whimsical, stylized, floral weights were all made *c.* 1850. They are typical of the Baccarat format of a single flower set within a garland of alternating complex canes, giving the whole a jewel-like appearance. Each of these examples includes in the garland an arrowhead assembly, consisting of eight arrowhead canes around a central fortress cane. This was a common combination in Baccarat weights. Note, also, the centers of the flower heads. The most common type used by Baccarat is the white stardust canes around a central red bull's-eye. The beautifully precise honeycomb cane center, with the tiny, hollow, six-pointed stars, is the next most often found. Both the wallflower and its central cane set-up are very rare. All except the red and white flower have a star-cut base to enhance their appearance.

BELOW
This **Whitefriars** weight was not
made as part of a limited edition as
a collector special, but it
nevertheless has the quality seen in
all Whitefriars products of the

period. The pastel-colored canes
are set flush into a translucent blue
ground, and a cane with a white
friar is included in the design,
together with the date 1978, two
years before the company closed.

ABOVE
This spaced concentric color
ground from **Clichy**, made *c.*1850,
has two concentric circles of
complex canes. The center is as
large a Clichy rose as you are likely
to see. Note how Clichy canes
resemble a lady's skirt viewed from
above, as they spread out towards
the base.

Today there are millions of glass paperweights. Most of these have been produced in quantity to sell inexpensively to the gift market. They are easily obtained from gift shops, and are generally regarded as colorful but mundane little baubles – something to brighten up the desk or shelf, but not to be taken seriously as collectibles. On the other hand, on June 26, 1990 a dealer paid $258,500 for a 19th-century French paperweight at Sotheby's, New York.

In this contrast lies one of the attractions of collecting paperweights. It is a hobby that can be pursued both by those with a limited budget and by those who are prepared to invest many thousands of dollars. There is no universal acceptance of the precise dividing line between what are known as "decorative" or "gift" paperweights and "collector" pieces. That is a judgement for each collector to make. But when the different kinds of paperweights are compared, the differences in terms of visual attraction and the skill that has gone into their making are clear to both novice and expert alike.

There is also a broad distinction between antique and modern paperweights, with those made in the 19th century regarded as antiques, while those made in the 20th

ABOVE
Strong, attractive colors as well as
exceptionally precise lampwork
are the features of this 1970s
weight by Paul Ysart. The two
stylized flowers, each with a bud,
are set perfectly flush into the
ground, which seems to be made
from small, blue glass chippings.
A *PY* signature-cane is included.

ABOVE
This nicely balanced study of dwarf
field pansies, made by studio artist
Paul Stankard in 1979, reflects the
attention to detail typical of the
artist. It includes three flowers,
each with fine purple markings,
one closed and one opening bud,
and a root system, which was a
unique feature of Stankard's work
at this time.

century are regarded as modern. Because of their historic interest and their scarcity, antique weights tend to command the highest prices at auction and with the dealers, but it is not age that determines collectibility. Some very fine paperweights are being produced today by both large companies and studio artists, and some of these will become the prized antiques of tomorrow.

Although its forms are predominantly utilitarian, and we see it in everyday use, most people recognize the visual attraction of glass. Even in its most basic forms, the medium lends itself ideally to artistic expression and elegance. Enthusiasts will claim that paperweights represent the ultimate attainment in glass artistry and craftsmanship. Compared with other forms of art glass, the paperweight makes greater use of refraction, providing images of the encased motifs that vary in size and aspect, and this adds an air of mystery for the viewer.

It is hoped that this book will whet the appetite of potential collectors. It is intended to be a guide to the different types and the principal makers, as well as including information on collecting.

It will not make you an expert, but it will take you some way along the road.

CHAPTER ONE

A Brief History of Paperweights

···· 19TH-CENTURY PAPERWEIGHTS····

Millefiori is the technique most commonly associated with paperweights, and its rediscovery and development in the 19th century led directly to the making of paperweights.

Millefiori uses patterned glass canes, which are drawn out to create miniaturized motifs. The precise origins of the technique are unknown, but we do know that it was used in Mesopotamia as early as the 15th century BC to decorate glass vessels. This early work was crude, but the craft developed, and by the 1st century AD detailed portrait canes had been produced in ancient Palestine and some fine glass mosaics had been made in Egypt. The Romans, too, used millefiori in the manufacture of decorative wall plaques, but after the fall of the Roman Empire, it seems that the craft was lost for a thousand years.

The first documentary reference we have is from the Venetian historian, Sabellico. Describing the glass industry of Murano, Venice, in 1494 he wrote a sentence that is carved firmly in the minds of all serious paperweight collectors: "But, consider to whom did it first occur to include in a little ball all the sorts of flowers which clothe the meadows in the Spring." He was referring

ABOVE

This Bohemian example, dated c.1845, has spaced complex canes including silhouettes set above a bed of white filigree canes. It is believed that Bohemian glass-makers could have been producing weights earlier than the French and that the French copied some of their patterns. This one certainly has its Baccarat and Clichy equivalents, although Clichy did not make silhouettes.

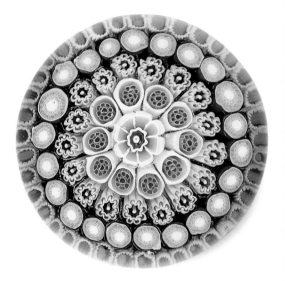

ABOVE

This fine concentric paperweight from Bacchus of Birmingham was made c.1851. The Bacchus craftsmen were masters in the use of colour, and although individual tones were not as strong as Clichy and tended to be predominantly pastel shades, the bright blue outer covering of one row of canes together with the use of white as a contrast gives this example a pleasing strength.

to solid glass balls containing millefiori, although these were not actually paperweights.

Little Venetian millefiori of this period seems to have survived, and it is possible that such as was produced was experimental and not exploited extensively as a commercial proposition. It appears that the craft was practised intermittently until 1833, when a more sustained revival of millefiori began with production by a factory in Silesia (now in Poland). During the next decade the craft was developed simultaneously in several European countries. From 1836 fine quality glass mosaics and millefiori canes were produced by Venetian craftsmen. These were intended primarily for use in jewellery, but they were also included in other articles. Some of these canes were exported to Bohemia (now part of the Czech Republic) where they were assembled with locally made components into high quality glassware.

It was around 1843 that a Venetian, Pietro Bigaglia, first made millefiori paperweights. He exhibited some at an international fair in 1845, and although documentary evidence seemed to imply that these exhibits inspired the French, this now seems unlikely. Venetian paperweights from this period that have survived are of a poor standard, being no more than haphazard assortments of canes, and they are totally out of keeping with the quality of other contemporary glassware, possibly because they were not taken

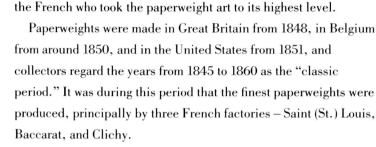

seriously. The French did, however, copy some of the Venetian cane types and mosaic designs, especially those by Giovanni Franchini and Domenico Bussolin. They may also have copied the paperweight format from Bohemian glassworkers, who were producing some excellent examples around this time, but it was the French who took the paperweight art to its highest level.

Paperweights were made in Great Britain from 1848, in Belgium from around 1850, and in the United States from 1851, and collectors regard the years from 1845 to 1860 as the "classic period." It was during this period that the finest paperweights were produced, principally by three French factories – Saint (St.) Louis, Baccarat, and Clichy.

  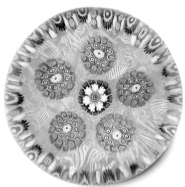

This was a time of great rivalry between international glass centers, and the main factories were continually looking for new techniques and lines to exploit. French entrepreneurs traveling in Europe carried information about the glass industries in Silesia, Bohemia, and Venice from the 1830s, and we must presume that they developed their own skills accordingly. From millefiori, they moved on to other glassmaking techniques, notably lampwork, so that they could then encapsulate a wide variety of other motifs in their own products.

Paperweights continued to be made in Europe until the late 1850s, and then for some unaccountable reason production ceased. Perhaps they simply fell from fashion. Throughout the remainder of the 19th century such paperweight activity as was pursued was spasmodic, but it was not without its high points. From c. 1878, for example, some paperweights were made at a fourth French factory, Cristalleries de Pantin, and these included some lizards, which are regarded by some as the greatest technical achievement in 19th-century paperweight manufacture, incorporating as they do landscapes with earth and plants.

LEFT

Writing in the 1981 annual bulletin of the PCA, Dwight P. Lanmon, director of the Corning Museum of Glass, stated that he considered the Pantin lizard or salamander weights represented the greatest technical achievements of 19th-century paperweight makers. There are 11 known examples, and only four have the type of construction of the weight shown here. It is made from a rod of glass, with overlays of yellow, green, and white on a colorless core. The scales are facets, cut through the overlays. It was made c.1878. (Photograph courtesy the Corning Museum of Glass)

Until recently, little was known of any Russian interest in paperweight production. Some floral lampworked paperweights and plaques of remarkably high quality were generally believed to have been the work of the Mount Washington Glass Co. in the United States. Evidence has now been produced that attributes the plaques, and by implication probably the paperweights, to Russian origin, although the date is unknown. In the United States, paperweight making started in 1851 and had a more continuous history, lasting until the 20th century. Because the industry was created by migrant glassworkers, mainly from France and England, the paperweights made in the 1850s and 1860s show strong European influences, although in general the quality falls far short of their European counterparts. In Europe the manufacture of paperweights was the result of commercial enterprise on the part of major factories, while in the United States it is more likely that it was a hobby for glassworkers, who were allowed to produce them after hours.

····20TH-CENTURY PAPERWEIGHTS····

By the turn of the century European influence on U.S. paperweights had diminished, and a new generation of craftsmen had developed their own styles. Among the most notable companies was Whitall Tatum Co., of Millville, New Jersey, which produced a distinctive type of rose weight from c. 1905.

ABOVE

One could be forgiven for assuming that this weight, in terms of colors, cane types, and design, came from the same factory as the Bacchus. This is not surprising, because it was made by the Gillinder factory, which was founded by William Gillinder (who worked for Bacchus before emigrating to the United States). It is possible that he took the silhouette of a lady with him from Bacchus.

LEFT
A Millville rose. This fully three-dimensional red rose was made 1905–12 by the Whitall Tatum Co. at Millville, New Jersey. A steel crimping tool shaped like a rose was used to push the colored glass into a gather of molten glass, and great skill was needed in subsequent working to achieve a good final shape. (Photograph courtesy the Corning Museum of Glass)

ABOVE
There are three types of Baccarat pansy, and this is not only the most common of the three, but is also the most often seen of all 19th-century floral weights, for which reason it is undeservedly undervalued. Considerable effort went into the making. Note, for example, how precisely the little black veins have been placed above the yellow petals, a feature, incidentally, that you will not see on the Dupont copy, left.

ABOVE
This Dupont pansy was made in the early 1930s. Note the muddy yellow coloring compared with the real 19th-century example. Baccarat almost invariably left a white edge to one of the large, upper petals to separate the two visually. It is absent from this copy. Although this is a lesser article than the original, it is clear that M. Dupont was a competent craftsman, and his work is collectible.

ABOVE
This brightly colored Bohemian example dates from the early 20th century. These weights were typically upright, stylized flowers of simple design, enhanced by a great variety of faceting. Note that the flower stems are formed of elongated air bubbles, which were made by inserting a metal pin into the hot glass during working.

Between 1900 and 1930, paperweights were again made in Bohemia. These were quite different from their 19th-century forebears, lacking the original quality but made attractive through generous faceting. These are generally referred to as "late Bohemian."

In France from 1931 to 1934, paperweights were made by a Baccarat craftsman, Dupont, who copied the antique Baccarat style of millefiori and pansy weights. From time to time these weights appear on the market, masquerading as 19th-century items. Their quality is very good, but experienced collectors can tell the difference.

In Britain, there was some paperweight activity from *c.* 1914 until 1951. The cane types, coloring, and style of this production are very similar to those of so-called 19th-century paperweights, previously attributed to Whitefriars or to the area of Stourbridge near Birmingham, in central England. Whitefriars, which was founded in 1680, produced paperweights from the 1930s until its closure in 1980. These may have been the first British weights made specifically for the collector market, because many were in the form of numbered limited editions.

In 1932, Paul Ysart, a member of a family of Spanish immigrant glassworkers in Scotland, began to produce paperweights as a hobby, but over the years they came to dominate his other glass work. The paperweights were signed with a *PY* cane, and as they found their way into collections, they were regarded as something of a mystery, for their source was unknown, although they showed great technical merit. Ysart was the first 20th-century paperweight maker to rediscover some of the lost skills of the 19th century, and he created fine pieces in the French manner while retaining a personal style. He was the major force behind the emergence of a substantial Scottish paperweight industry.

In the United States, in the meantime, Charles Kaziun began to make glass buttons and paperweights from *c.* 1942. Kaziun is generally recognized as the first of the quality "studio artists" – those who work alone with a modern furnace, producing paperweights and related articles in a variety of ways, including crimped flowers, lampwork, and millefiori.

Until this time in the 20th century, paperweight making was spasmodic and scattered. Collecting was predominantly concerned with 19th-century examples, and was the province of the wealthy. A 20th-century paperweight renaissance was driven by the

ABOVE
This early bouquet from Paul Ysart shows a style that is quite distinct from the traditional French weights of the classic period. The canes are rather basic and the floral lampwork had not reached the precise standard he later developed, but the overall effect is colorful and pleasing, and at the time no contemporary work of comparable quality existed.

ABOVE
A Charles Kaziun version of the Millville rose. Made in 1946–48, this is unusual for its blue color, but is typical of Kaziun's immaculate quality. (Photograph courtesy the Corning Museum of Glass)

American entrepreneur, Paul Jokelson, who had a strong interest in sulfides and paperweights. In 1952 he persuaded the French factories of Baccarat and St. Louis to begin making sulfide paperweights, and he operated as a distributor, having exclusive U.S. rights for St. Louis and Paul Ysart. In 1953 he formed the Paperweight Collectors Association (P.C.A.). By the late 1950s Baccarat and St. Louis had extended their ranges to millefiori, and St. Louis was experimenting with lampwork, but it was not until the late 1960s that both factories began to use these techniques to produce fine collector weights. It is interesting to reflect that these two great glass houses, both with enviable historical records, took 15 years or so to attain a standard that was in some respects still short of what their predecessors accomplished in 10 years, despite the 19th-century examples on which they could model their efforts.

The growing interest and a developing market in the United States led to the appearance of a number of studio artists, who followed the example of Charles Kaziun, although they tended to confine their efforts to lampworked subjects and avoided millefiori. Specialized dealers began to promote the business in general and the new artists in particular, and the whole paperweight business became a viable commercial enterprise.

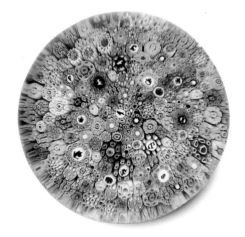

ABOVE
Inspired by their 19th-century predecessors, 20th-century Baccarat craftsmen produced this close millefiori paperweight, complete with silhouettes, in 1968. The difference is that the silhouettes are not Gridel animals, but the signs of the zodiac.

ABOVE
This colorful flat bouquet of stylized flowers, made by St. Louis in 1981, is a copy of a well-known St Louis antique. The keen-eyed will spot the *SL1981* cane in the center of the white flower so that there will be no misunderstanding of its true age.

ABOVE
This elegant and simple fuchsia is by Francis Whittemore, one of the first of the U.S. studio artists. He has used bright colors against a dark green ground to create a luminous subject, and has made it appear three-dimensional by shading the flower. It was made in the early 1970s.

The rich blue ground enhances the effect of this 1982 weight with nursery-rhyme and cartoon character silhouettes from Perthshire Paperweights. Perthshire has made silhouettes something of a specialty, and it is, to date, the only 20th-century maker to produce multicolored ones, which it first introduced for sale in 1973.

First Quarter. This excellent version of a new moon above the Earth demonstrates the break with traditional designs sought by Colin Terris and Peter Holmes at Caithness Glass. This example was made by Peter Holmes in 1976 as part of a limited edition of 1,500.

Dealers and collectors were keen to look beyond their local sources of supply. Paul Jokelson had started both the French and Scottish connections, and the latter, stimulated by U.S. demand, began to grow at a considerable pace. Paul Ysart continued to make paperweights, and through training and example he left a trail of expertise in the companies in which he worked. In 1968 Perthshire Paperweights was formed by Stuart Drysdale, a Scottish lawyer and paperweight enthusiast. This was the first ever factory to be dedicated to making paperweights, and the first collector items were made in 1969 in the traditional French manner, using millefiori and lampwork techniques. In 1969 Caithness Glass started to make paperweights with abstract themes, using arrangements of bubbles and colored glass fragments. The artists charting this direction were Colin Terris and Peter Holmes, both of whom had worked under the guidance of Paul Ysart. In the late 1970s, Peter Holmes set up his own works at Selkirk, trading as Selkirk Glass.

The impact of the Scottish factories on collecting and its general image was fundamental, for they recognized that they could not devote themselves entirely to limited quantities of expensive collector weights if they were to be financially viable. There had always been a demand for low-cost trinkets, and in the field of paperweights this market had been served for many years by the thousands of colorful items made in China and Murano. The Scottish factories produced a range of inexpensive but good quality "gift weights," which they supplemented by the collector specials, made in limited quantities. The problem with paperweights from China and Murano is that they lead nowhere. In contrast, there must be many collectors who started with a low-cost Caithness or Perthshire weight, and then moved up the scale as they grew to appreciate what was available from these and other manufacturers.

In recent years the main centers of paperweight production have followed different paths. European makers improved their quality during the 1970s, reaching a high standard that was based essentially on traditional techniques and designs. In the United States, on the other hand, developments had followed different lines. The artist Paul Stankard set the definitive standard in lampwork technique. He produced botanical subjects of considerable delicacy and of an accuracy unprecedented in this medium, and other artists are continuing to take new directions in subject matter and technique.

RIGHT

A perfectly executed trillium by Paul Stankard. This was made in 1980, by which time Stankard's work had matured to an unrivaled level. He has included the root ball, stamens, and realistic twists to the red-veined white petals, and his artistic presentations of subjects like this always seem best set in clear glass.

ABOVE

Fruit was a specialty of the late Delmo Tarsitano, and his peaches were probably the most realistic. The texture of this 1983 example makes it look good enough to eat.

RIGHT

This bird landscape shows the work of U.S. artist Rick Ayotte at its best. It seems incredible that it is made entirely of glass, as the textures of the leaves, twigs of the nest, and even the feathers on the bird are all faithfully reproduced. Made in 1987, this is a masterpiece of modern lampwork.

As collectors' interest grows and the availability of the antiques diminishes, it is reassuring that a new generation of paperweight artists is continuing the tradition and seeking new standards of excellence in this most challenging area of glass art.

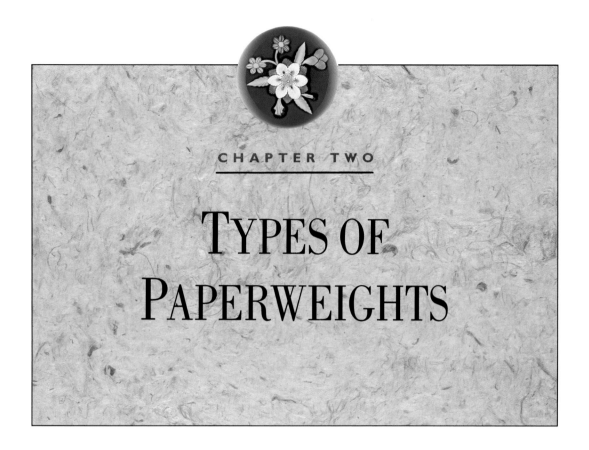

CHAPTER TWO

TYPES OF PAPERWEIGHTS

The most important advice for a new collector is to gain a knowledge of the wide scope of paperweights available. Accordingly, of all the sections in this book, this one dealing with types has been given the greatest space. Nevertheless, this book cannot and does not seek to be totally comprehensive – no book on paperweights yet published has accomplished that task, which would require more than a single volume. The intention is to cover the more important and most frequently encountered types and their makers, with a few rarities thrown in for good measure.

COLLECTOR VERSUS GIFT PAPERWEIGHTS

Before looking at the main types of paperweight, it is important to distinguish between collector and gift weights. Over the years hundreds of thousands of low-cost paperweights have been produced, at two centers in particular, China and Murano, Venice. This flood has given paperweights their general poor image, and the chances are that your first encounter with a paperweight was with one of these.

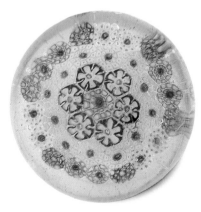

ABOVE

The yellow cast to the glass and its exceptionally shallow dome are the tell-tale signs of its Chinese origin. Weights like this began to be made in the early 1930s, and although they are of indifferent quality, the canework is better than more recent exports from China. Because they now have an historic interest, Chinese paperweights have become collectible.

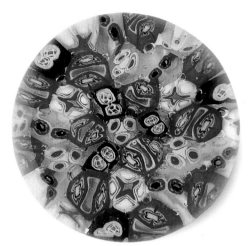

ABOVE
A close millefiori Chinese weight
made in the 1970s. Notice how the
quality of canework has
deteriorated since the 1930s.

Paperweights have been made in China since the 1930s. Some early examples were pictorial, but the designs were mostly based on French millefiori. Their quality was poor, and the glass had a yellowy tinge and lacked clarity. Since the 1950s and 1960s the quality of the glass has improved, but the workmanship has not. Chinese paperweights are easily identified. They invariably have a flat but unpolished base, and the coloring is bright, with lots of yellow and orangy-reds. Millefiori canes are simple, poorly formed, and untidily arranged, and bubbles are frequently present. Chinese floral weights, although inexpensive and of limited technical merit, have a more pleasing appearance. They are usually upright and three-dimensional, with large petals. Another frequently seen type is like a sea anemone.

The products of Murano are better quality, but in the main they are produced as inexpensive souvenirs. The base of the weight is nearly always flat and polished. Millefiori canes are basic and not always precisely formed, although some better canes can be found – those attributed to Moretti, for example. Sometimes ambitious designs are attempted, but they rarely succeed, and in general the workmanship is only moderate.

The Chinese and Muranese weights illustrated here are typical, and although they do not occupy an important place in collecting, it is important for the beginner to be able to recognize them. They

ABOVE
This bright red, footed flower is superior to most Chinese weights. It is not really in the collector category, but it certainly brightens up the room.

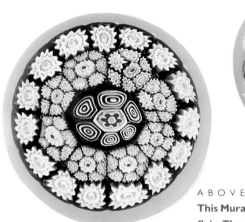

ABOVE
Millefiori weights from Murano are usually easily identifiable. Note the coarse, white, cogged appearance of the canes, which are very typical.

ABOVE
This Murano crown shows more flair. The crown is relatively well made, but has been spoiled by the unsympathetic cane set-up on top.

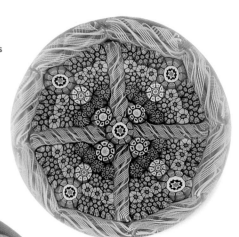

Perthshire Paperweights produces a limited edition each year with more to the design and more complex canes. This one of 250 made in 1985 is a good starting point for the new collector.

A basic but good quality gift weight by Perthshire Paperweights. This type is regarded by the factory as its "bread and butter" because of the high volume sales they achieve.

A fine collector special, this cockerel cushion weight is one of 334 made in 1977. The large cockerel silhouette can be seen through the circular aperture in the red cushion.

A unique weight of a type made only by Perthshire Paperweights. This is a double overlay encased within a double overlay. The simple motif of three stylized roses is placed on a white circular tablet. After encapsulation in clear glass, this is overlaid with a covering of ruby on white. The overlay is then cut to leave the petal-like structures surrounding the motif. The whole is first encased in clear glass, then overlaid in ruby on white, then cut with a double row of windows and a large viewing aperture on top.

frequently appear at antique fairs and run-of-the-mill antique shops, purporting to be antiques, and often with prices out of all proportion to their real value.

Gift weights are made virtually everywhere there is a glass industry, and it is impossible to determine the origins of many of them. It is up to collectors to judge the desirability of these items once they are familiar with the range of quality available. There is no better designation of collector and gift weights than that provided by Perthshire Paperweights of Scotland. This factory markets its products in four distinct categories: gift weights, regular annual collector patterns in limited quantities, half a dozen collector specials each year, and a few one-of-a-kind items. The illustrations here, which show an example of each, clearly reflect the different levels.

···················· M I L L E F I O R I ····················

Millefiori is the technique generally associated with paperweights. The name derives from the Italian for "thousands of flowers," which is the overall impression created by the hundreds of colored glass canes packed closely together. The motif of a millefiori paperweight is a patterned arrangement of canes, which are of four basic types: solid (single-color rods), patterned, spiral twists, and silhouettes.

Patterned canes can be made in several ways, but the most usual is the use of molds. A steel pontil rod is used to take a gather of semi-molten colored glass from the furnace and press it down into a mold, which could, for example, be in the shape of a star. The star-shaped gather is then withdrawn and another rod attached, so that the two craftsmen involved back away from each other to pull the glass to a length of 30 feet or more. The drawn-out cane retains its shape, although in diminished size, and it is broken into convenient lengths for further processing. Bundles of such canes, which are used with a further gather of clear or colored glass, are reheated, pressed into another mold, and drawn out to produce a complex patterned cane. If the process is repeated, tiny pattern elements, barely visible to the naked eye, are formed. Finished canes are sliced into cross sections for assembly into the patterns for the paperweight.

ABOVE

A modern masterpiece from St. Louis. In 1978, at the request of the Corning Museum of Glass, St. Louis produced 300 magnum encased overlays, 150 upright bouquets, and 150 close millefiori mushrooms. This is one of the mushrooms. Making these paperweights was a challenge to see if the craftsmen of today could repeat the achievement of their 19th-century predecessors.

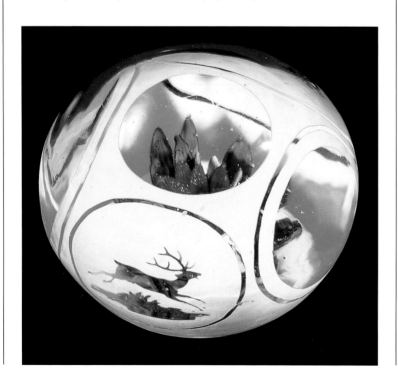

LEFT

An antique masterpiece from St. Louis, this encased overlay was made between 1845 and 1855. During that period, St. Louis always featured upright bouquets in this type of weight, which is extremely rare, especially in this engraved form. Given the present-day experience of producing encased overlays, with the necessary days of processing and high risks of spoilage, one wonders whether St. Louis made these pieces more as prestige items to demonstrate the skills of the craftsmen than as a profitable selling line. The few examples that have survived seem to support that view. (Photograph courtesy the Corning Museum of Glass)

Spiral twists are made from slender rods of white or colored glass together with clear glass. The rods are placed vertically into a mold, and then a clear glass gather is inserted into the mold. Rotating the cane while it is being drawn out produces the spiral, and the results of the technique are known as "filigree." Filigree was developed by the Venetians in the 16th century, and it is well known in other Venetian glass products. It was also used in a variety of patterns in the stems of drinking glasses made in Britain from *c.* 1755 to 1780.

Silhouette canes resemble little pictures, and they can be single or multicolored. Molds can be used to produce simple silhouettes, but more complex ones, which are made in the manner of antique portrait canes, involve the assembly of many slender glass rods into a mosaic, which is then fused to make a single cane. During the 19th century, French craftsmen used the different kinds of cane to produce an ingenious variety of millefiori arrangements, a tradition that is being continued by some of today's factories.

CLOSE MILLEFIORI

The close millefiori design is one of the most popular types, and most collections will include at least one example. The canes are packed tightly and in a random formation in a mound, which is ideally set fairly low in the dome in order to get the best from the magnification. In most paperweights some canes will be repeated, but a good example will contain hundreds, implying hundreds of processes in the making. The better examples will be packed so that there are no large gaps between the canes and no bubbles. A good, close millefiori will look solid, and opaque, and this appearance will sometimes be accomplished by mounting the canes on a colored ground.

A close millefiori weight can look untidy when it is viewed from the side unless special care is taken. Cane slices are usually of varying thickness, and the underside of the outer row can appear ragged and uneven. The most usual method of dealing with this problem is to use longer canes, and to draw the outer row underneath the weight to form a kind of basket. In the 19th century Clichy craftsmen went a stage further — they used an outer row of canes, alternating white with a color. Some Bohemian weights are in the same style, and it is possible that the idea actually originated in Bohemia.

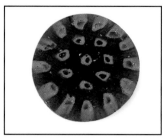

ABOVE

By the time this Roman button was made, possibly 900 or so years ago, millefiori had been established as a craft for over 1,500 years.

BELOW

This Strathearn example is from the late 1960s. The canes are fairly simple, but the whole is very colorful. Because of their moderate cost, Strathearn weights are popular with collectors.

ABOVE

Three different interpretations of the close millefiori type are shown here. Left: Baccarat; middle: Clichy; and right: Strathearn. The Baccarat example is an exercise in fine, precise canework. There is a multitude of cane types, showing great variety in design, and these are recognized by experienced collectors and used as a means of identification. The overall effect is pleasing, especially to those who like intricate detail. Nevertheless, despite its quality and unquestionable popularity among collectors, it ranks behind the Clichy version in overall appeal. At first sight the Clichy canes appear to be less complex than the Baccarat ones, but close examination shows that this is not so. Clichy canes seem to have been made in an almost infinite variety of patterns, and they are packed tightly together to give the impression of a basket of flowers. The Baccarat canes, on the other hand, seem to stand out as individuals, an effect heightened by the frequent small gaps between them. Taken on its own, the Strathearn example, which was made *c*.1970, would appear a competent and attractive piece of work. Comparing it with the two 19th-century models puts it into perspective.

In 19th-century Baccarat close millefiori weights the canes are formed almost into a ball, so that when they are viewed from the side, the cross section is still visible. The canes are drawn under only at the base, leaving a small hole in the center through which it can be seen that pieces of filigree are enclosed within the cane ball, presumably to increase the opacity, such was the care taken in those days to achieve the desired result.

In addition to the qualities already mentioned, close millefiori paperweights should have a good overall color and a varied assortment of complex, precisely formed canes, with a minimum of obvious duplication. The canes should also be set vertically, with none slanting out of line with the rest.

CONCENTRIC MILLEFIORI

A concentric millefiori design consists of a number of concentric rings of canes set around a central cane or complex arrangement of canes. In a close concentric paperweight, the rings are packed closely together; in an open concentric weight, they are apart. This is one of the most common types of millefiori paperweight.

Sometimes the canes will simply be encased in clear glass – that is, they will not be set over a contrasting ground. This is appropriate for a close concentric, but for an open concentric a good ground is necessary to enhance the appearance so that the canes do not appear to be suspended in space. A base of colored glass is a simple and effective way of producing a contrasting ground. Colored glass is translucent, which is how the ground will sometimes appear. To make a color opaque, it must be coated over white glass, and a cane pattern is occasionally mounted on opaque white. Such a weight is termed a sodden snow.

In the 19th century it seems to have been difficult to position the canes precisely, but good quality control today should ensure that modern weights are not marred by this deficiency. Placing canes in their pattern is now done by hand assembly into a metal jig early in the process, and a gather of glass is pressed onto the assembled canes so that they stick to it. Some skill is needed to ensure that in the subsequent working of the glass, including its journeys into the furnace, the canes retain their original position.

In concentric millefiori paperweights, the complexity and precision of the individual canes are less important than the quality of the colors and the way in which they are combined.

SCATTERED MILLEFIORI

A scattered millefiori design consists of random canes spaced apart. In the simplest form of the pattern they are set in clear glass, but, as with open concentric weights, the canes look more effective if they are above a ground. Scattered millefiori weights can be extremely striking when there is a contrasting ground, so that the complex canes stand out as specimens. For this reason, collectors insist that the individual canes in this particular type of weight are of the finest quality and complexity. The color ground in this and other forms was a particular success of the Clichy factory, and the most popular paperweights have an attractive near-turquoise ground.

ABOVE
A Clichy paperweight of spaced canes on sodden snow dating from c.1850. This type of weight is generally of poor quality, with the often out-of-position canes contributing to the indifferent appearance. This example happens to be better than average, with the strong, contrasting colors standing out well against the white background. Despite the random appearance, it is actually a four-ringed concentric pattern.

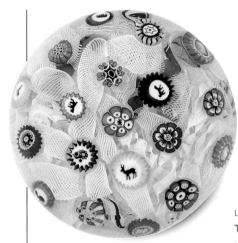

The Baccarat spaced canes on upset muslin include *B1848* signature and date-cane. This is a near-perfect example of the type, with the small strips of colored ribbon providing added interest.

ABOVE
This Clichy chequer, made *c.*1850, is of outstanding quality. Notice how the canes are made more distinctive by the separating strips of filigree. To give a little more substance to these weights, Clichy used to lay parallel strips of filigree underneath the canes.

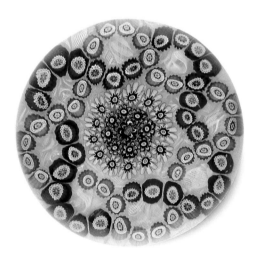

ABOVE
This garland weight is typical of the Clichy quality, especially in its orderly arrangement. Two quatrefoil garlands are set above a ground of upset muslin. Parallel strips of filigree are laid underneath to increase the weight's overall opacity.

Another successful style used in the 19th century was to set spaced canes above jumbled pieces of filigree, and the term coined to describe this feature was "upset muslin." If the filigree is very bright white, the specimen canes stand out superbly. Clichy made a number of these, but by far the best were made by Baccarat. When the filigree is laid in strips between the canes, the weight is called a chequer, and this was a specialty of the Clichy factory. Although Baccarat made a few chequer weights, these were different, in that the divisions between the canes were simply blue strips of glass – rather than spiral twists.

When the filigree is laid in strips between the canes, and it is white with a twist of color, the weight is called a barber pole. Such weights were made by Clichy and are fairly rare, commanding much higher prices than basic chequers.

GARLAND PAPERWEIGHTS

A garland weight has strings of similar canes. There is a great diversity of garland types, but the most common have two entwined garlands. Garlands with three loops are called trefoil, and those with four, quatrefoil.

Extremely complex canes are not so essential for garlands, which benefit more from orderly arrangement, attractive color combinations, and a contrasting ground. In the 19th century, the Clichy factory produced the greatest number and variety of garland weights. They are also the most highly regarded.

RIGHT
A Baccarat Dupont garland made in the early 1930s. This weight, which has two trefoil garlands, is well made, but the canes are not special, and the overall appearance does not compare with its 19th-century equivalents.

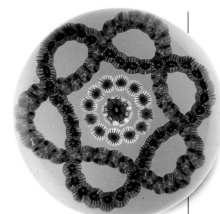

CARPET GROUND

A weight that appears as a carpet of simple, identical canes on which has been placed the motif or pattern is known as a carpet ground. In fact, the pattern is often set among the carpet canes. Carpet grounds are among the most attractive of millefiori paperweights, for the carpet generally appears more effective than either color grounds or upset muslin. Antique examples are very rare, much sought after, and command exceptionally high prices. Fortunately, modern versions are more reasonably priced, and the quality of some is impeccable. Many modern examples rival the antique ones in craftsmanship, if not in color.

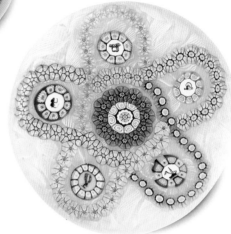

ABOVE
A charming garland weight made by Perthshire Paperweights to a design based on the antique Baccarat type, which was rarely produced in a double overlay form. This example, which was made in 1980, uses soft colors to create the attractive overall appearance, while the precise assembly and quaint little silhouette canes exude superior quality.

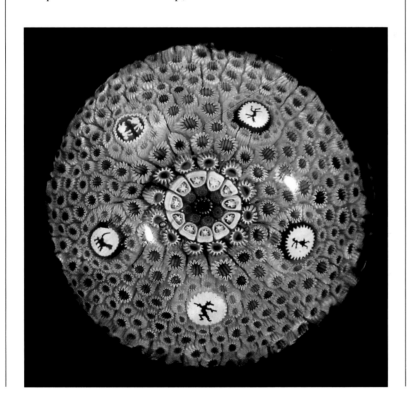

LEFT
This fine example of an antique St. Louis carpet ground is a gem, and would be out of reach of most collectors. Five must have been a magic number for St. Louis, because this arrangement of five canes or set-ups around a central one is almost a trademark of the company. (Photograph courtesy the Corning Museum of Glass)

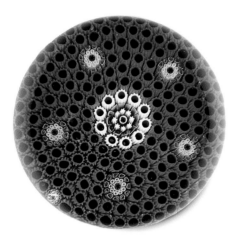

ABOVE
This St. Louis carpet ground was made in 1986, and is more in keeping with the company's 19th-century style, with its carpet of hollow-cogged canes. The cane arrangement also shows that old habits die hard – the five canes around a central set-up are clearly visible here.

LEFT
This contrast in color and design from Perthshire Paperweights was made in 1977. This carpet ground contains seven tiny, multicolored silhouette canes.

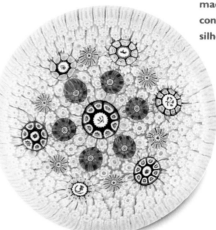

ABOVE
This concentric St. Louis mushroom with torsade, made c.1850, is a typical example – the perfectly shaped mushroom has a good color combination, but there are some uneven rings of canes.

MUSHROOM PAPERWEIGHTS

The millefiori mushroom is one of the most fascinating styles. The long canes are drawn underneath to form a stem, which in modern weights tends to taper to a point, while the head of the mushroom shows the canes in either close millefiori or close concentric formation. Only the better makers are able to produce a good mushroom, and today some excellent examples are being made. The head pattern of a good mushroom will conform to the criteria for close millefiori or close concentric. It will be well formed and symmetrical, and the edge of the head will be circular and even. It will also stand upright and not slanted. Antique mushrooms made by Baccarat and St. Louis were often enhanced by the addition of a torsade around the base of the stalk. A torsade, sometimes called a twist ring, is a circular filigree cane with a colored twist around it. No modern manufacturer has yet been able to make a mushroom with a torsade successfully.

PANEL PAPERWEIGHTS

Sometimes the pattern is divided into a number of panels, each of which will usually contain similar canes. The panels may be divided by rows of identical canes, or by filigree canes laid laterally, as spokes radiating from the center. In the 19th century, all three of the main French factories made panel weights, and the Baccarat ones in particular are of magnificent quality and appearance.

ABOVE
This Baccarat close millefiori mushroom with torsade, dating from c.1850, is of a fairly common type for the company, but they only rarely contained silhouette canes. The central cane in this weight is, therefore, a bonus. Notice the very fine filigree in the torsade.

ABOVE
St. Louis sometimes used jasper grounds for floral weights, but the chips were more finely ground. The coarser version, shown in this example from c.1850, was always used for the panel weights, and it somehow seems more suited to the type.

RIGHT
St. Louis made this mushroom in 1981. Usually a double overlay is formed from a color on white, but here an interesting effect is created by overlaying white on green. This is one area in which modern techniques have improved on the antiques – the mushroom is well formed, and the concentric rings are perfectly arranged.

The St. Louis factory produced two very different types of panel weight. The first is called a cruciform, because it consists of a cross made of laterally laid filigree. The four segments are filled with an assortment of canes in symmetrical patterns.

The second type is called a jasper ground panel. It is made up of a number of white spokes radiating from the center, each segment having a speckled ground called jasper. The panels are alternately colored, usually blue and white and red and white, and a complex cane is placed at each of the interstices at the center. The intriguing feature of St. Louis jasper ground panels is that they invariably have a torsade encircling the weight, but it is set so low that it is not visible from ordinary viewing, and the extra effort involved adds nothing to the appearance.

PIÉDOUCHE PAPERWEIGHTS

A piédouche (pedestal) weight is similar to a mushroom, but the head, stem, and footed base are not further encased in glass – that is, the whole is actually shaped like a mushroom. The stem is often composed of filigree canes or of latticinio, which give a basket-like appearance. Piédouche weights require considerable craft skill, and antique examples are prohibitively expensive.

CROWN PAPERWEIGHTS

A crown is made up of alternate color twist and filigree canes, which run in lengths from the top to the bottom of the weight, just like lines of longitude on a globe. A color twist cane consists of two colors separated by white, resulting in a ribbon-like appearance.

In the 19th century, crowns were made in Bohemia and in the United States, but the most famous and the best were made by the St. Louis factory. Antique St. Louis crowns are hollow, which is,

ABOVE

This little crown by John Deacons is probably one of the best bargains around for collectors. It is beautifully made and, unusually for a modern crown, all the staves are nicely perpendicular, the result of a special shaping technique unique to this maker. It was made in 1991, when it cost $75.

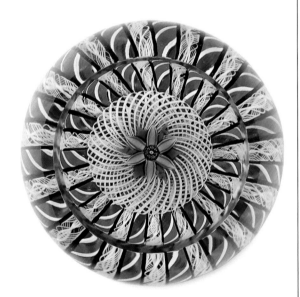

ABOVE

Perthshire Paperweights chose a crown like this for the cover of the book about the factory, and with good reason. The crown is well formed, with double-twist filigree canes, and it has been further enhanced by a fine piece of latticinio on top, with a stylized, lampworked flower in the center. A large, concave facet on top completes the weight, of which just 191 were made in 1981.

perhaps, one reason they appear superior compared with the solid, 20th-century versions. St. Louis crowns are usually of good, strong colors, the canes usually being red, green, and blue with white. The manufacturing process always results in an untidy junction at the top, and this is overcome by placing a complex cane at this point. One problem that makers cannot always solve is how to keep the staves perpendicular. Although they start that way in the special funnel-shaped jig, the rotation during the shaping process tends to slant them. This is an important point to check when buying this type of weight.

SCRAMBLED PAPERWEIGHTS

Paperweights that consist of a jumbled assortment of canes and cane fragments encased in clear glass are known as scrambled weights. They are sometimes called "end-of-day" weights, because it is assumed that they were put together after work in order not to waste the residual glass. It seems that in the 1840s the Baccarat factory was somewhat formal in everything it did, and in keeping with the precision of its mainstream millefiori canes and designs, it could not bring itself to relax its standards even after hours – the filigree canes in Baccarat scrambleds are laid in crisscross fashion at right angles.

MAJOR
······MILLEFIORI MANUFACTURERS······

Up till now millefiori paperweights have been discussed in terms of 19th-century manufacture. This is inevitable because it was the craftsmen of that period who originated the principal types. In the 20th century, attempts have been made to develop some original styles, but in the main the basic formats have remained unchanged. The following discussion of the principal makers will, therefore, also concentrate on the 19th rather than the 20th century, although more recent developments are included.

CLICHY

The Clichy factory, known at the time as Maës of Clichy-la-Garenne, made mostly millefiori weights. It is generally accepted that Clichy paperweights have the better colors, and that type for type they are superior to those produced by their competitors, a sentiment that seems to be echoed in the saleroom today. There is,

RIGHT

Two trefoil interlaced garlands on a bright blue ground produce the striking effect for which Clichy was renowned in the 19th century. No other factory produced garlands of this quality.

ABOVE

The crisscross canes in this Baccarat scrambled weight from c.1850 are not quite as well ordered as usual, but they have obviously been placed more tidily than the scrambleds made in other factories.

nevertheless, a great variability in the quality and intrinsic merit of Clichy paperweights – only a minority is truly great, while there are a number of high quality desirables and many simple, basic types. The most common styles are scattered canes in clear glass and open concentrics with a central cane, an inner ring of similar canes, and an outer ring of five or six large canes, interspersed with pairs of smaller canes. There must be thousands of this particular type in existence, and it must have been one of the company's staple products, corresponding to the Perthshire gift category today.

Although Clichy produced a seemingly infinite variety of complex canes, it used the simpler ones for its volume production, but with one notable exception – the Clichy rose. The Clichy rose resembles a rosebud from which the top has been sliced. The cane type seems to have been invented by Giovanni Franchini of Venice, but it was used by most European makers in the 19th century. It was, however, used most frequently by Clichy, and, because it appears in probably more than half of all that company's millefiori weights, it has come to be regarded as its trademark. Although it occurs so often, a weight with a Clichy rose is always a little more desirable, and one with several roses is highly desirable, especially if they form a complete garland.

Overall, Clichy millefiori weights have a definite floral flavor, especially the close millefiori and close concentric styles, which convey the impression of a closely packed basket of flowers. Very

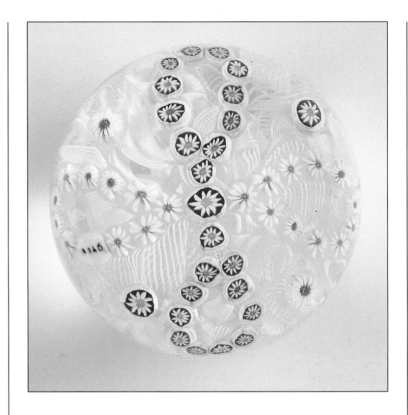

RIGHT AND BELOW

An unsuspecting observer might take the Dupont weight for an antique Baccarat, but the quality of a genuine Baccarat example is unmistakable. The Murano weight cheekily includes a 1846 date-cane in a weight that is not up to collector status. The best that can be said is that the maker got the period right.

RIGHT

A 20th-century present from Murano.

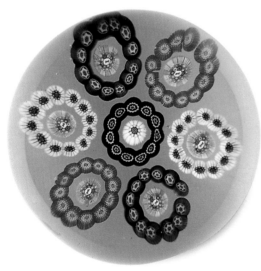

ABOVE

A Baccarat Dupont made in the early 1930s.

few Clichy weights were signed, but three methods are known to have been used. A C Scroll weight is one that has a number of garlands, each shaped as a letter *C*, facing towards the center. Very rarely, a cane with a letter *C* is included in the design. Such a signature will add greatly to the value. Rarest of all are weights that include canes depicting the full word *Clichy*.

The Clichy factory was taken over in 1885, and the company's tradition has not continued into the 20th century, although its influence in design and style persists.

BACCARAT

The Baccarat style is a direct contrast with Clichy. The company's millefiori weights have a less floral appearance, and more formality and precision. Individual canes, although no more complex than those used by Clichy, create an impression of greater complexity, and they look very geometric. The factory does not appear to have made simple and basic types for volume production. At the lowest level it produced garlands in clear glass, but even these have a well-organized quality that places them above the simple Clichy volume types. They often include garlands of white stardust canes, each cane consisting of a number of white stars.

ABOVE
Evidence of the consistent high quality of Baccarat's work, these three-dimensional yellow crocuses with their bright orange stamens are mounted on a white, chalky ground, and are an original and highly artistic subject. This weight was made in 1981.

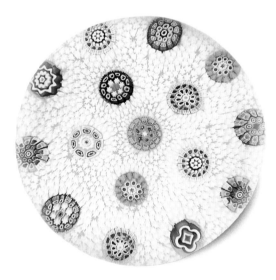

ABOVE
In the 19th century, Baccarat and Clichy made a few carpet grounds of scattered canes set among a carpet of white star canes. St. Louis made this outstanding example, with its exceptionally fine, complex canes, in 1982.

Baccarat made a large number of consistently high quality close millefiori, scattered millefiori on upset muslin, and close millefiori mushrooms, all of which are keenly collected. Most of the close millefiori and scattered millefiori contain a cane with the letter *B* over a date. The dates most often seen, in descending order of frequency, are 1848, 1847, 1849, and 1846; exceptionally rare are 1853 and 1858.

An almost universal feature of these two types is the inclusion of silhouette canes. The silhouettes are nearly always black against a white background or white against a colored background, and they are mainly animal subjects. Baccarat carpet grounds are very rare, of high quality, and consequently extremely expensive.

Today paperweights are a very small part of Baccarat's output, but, as is to be expected from this renowned maker of fine crystal, they are of high quality. The millefiori ones are traditional in design, being mainly close millefiori, concentrics, carpet grounds, and mushrooms. In the 1970s, Baccarat produced a series, including silhouette canes, based on its own 19th-century designs. Subsequently it created silhouette canes featuring the signs of the zodiac, which were incorporated into close millefiori or carpet grounds up to 1989. Baccarat produces only a few weights each year, and since 1992, according to its promotional brochures, has made just one millefiori type each year in a quantity of 150.

ST. LOUIS

The St. Louis factory produced a number of fairly basic types, which even today ought not to be prohibitively expensive. The simplest are a single complex cane or a central set-up, both on a jasper ground. The next simplest is a central cane set-up surrounded by five spaced cane set-ups. St. Louis specialized in close concentrics, concentric mushrooms with torsades, and the very rare carpet grounds. At some stage there seems to have been difficulty in maintaining a tidy arrangement of canes because they frequently appear out of position, which is an obvious fault in a concentric design. In others, albeit the minority, they are neatly in place. A few irregularities seem to be tolerated by collectors, because the values appear to be little affected by these faults.

Individually, St. Louis colors are inferior to those of Clichy, but this deficiency is offset by skillful combinations, which have resulted in some beautiful weights. Cane types are fairly similar to those of Baccarat, but there is a greater use of canes that look like

ABOVE
George Bacchus & Sons, a Birmingham company, made paperweights on a limited scale from 1848, and of these the most common were close concentrics. Although the canes were less sophisticated than in French or Bohemian examples, and the colors were not as strong, Bacchus succeeded in producing a good overall effect, partly through the choice of color combinations and partly through the greater depth, which was achieved by using longer canes, drawn right down to the base.

ABOVE
The Whitefriars' Christmas weight of 1975, featuring 13 angel silhouettes.

cogwheels. St. Louis also made silhouette canes, although less often than Baccarat.

Concentric mushrooms are almost invariably enhanced by the inclusion of a torsade encircling the stem. This is more often than not a cane of white filigree with a bright blue twist around it. The filigree is fairly thick and coarse compared with the exceptionally fine Baccarat torsade, but it achieves a better visual effect. Rarely, the torsade will have a pink or a yellowy-orange twist instead of the blue, and these weights will command higher prices. St. Louis carpet grounds are not desperately rare, but they are keenly sought after and highly valued. The usual format includes spaced silhouette canes, and the carpet will more often than not be of the cogwheel-type cane.

The company has been producing limited edition millefiori weights since 1970, mostly in traditional designs, but occasionally introducing new patterns. The canes and cane assemblies are beautifully precise, with the carpet grounds and mushrooms being near perfect. Canes can be quite complex, but so far no silhouettes have been made in the 20th century.

········· BRITISH MANUFACTURERS ·········

Of 19th-century British production, the weights attributed to George Bacchus & Sons of Birmingham are most in favor with collectors today, and are generally accepted as being of the best quality. They are very rare, and only two or three hundred are believed to have been made from 1848. Types of paperweights made are close millefiori, close concentric, spaced on sodden snow, and mushrooms.

Bacchus weights, which use pastel colors, usually have a softer appearance than French millefiori examples.

Apart from a few surviving weights made by the Islington Glass Works, the other 19th-century British-made paperweights provide an unsolved mystery, and are the subject of much controversy in paperweight circles.

For many years paperweights, crudely made compared with the French and mainly close concentrics, using simple, brightly colored canes, were variously attributed to the long-established Whitefriars glassworks or to the glass-producing area of Stourbridge, near Birmingham. Sometimes 1848 date-canes were included in the design.

ABOVE

Apart from the cane type and the identifying cane of a white friar included in the design, these weights can be recognized by the base. A deep, circular groove shows how the weight consists of two pieces that have been welded together – the internal piece is the one with the canes – and only Whitefriars weights have this distinctive characteristic.

RIGHT

This Whitefriars concentric weight from the 1930s is similar in style and coloring to paperweights that have been attributed to Whitefriars' 19th-century production. In common with those paperweights, it lacks the quality of the later Whitefriars products.

In 1987, an English dealer, John Smith, wrote an article – "The Myth of Whitefriars" – for the annual bulletin of the Paperweight Collectors' Association of the United States in which he claimed that there was no documentary evidence that Whitefriars made paperweights before 1930, despite the existence of a great many company records. Smith also unearthed a letter written in 1960 from a man who claimed that between 1928 and 1951, while working for a company, John Walsh-Walsh Ltd., he was required to make paperweights with 1848 dates in them. There have since been some vigorous rebuttals of this article, but more recent research by Roger Dodsworth of the Broadfield House Museum near Birmingham, England, has unearthed pattern-books of H. G. Richardson dated 1914 and 1915, depicting paperweights and ink bottles in the Whitefriars style. There is, therefore, clear evidence of production by at least two British companies between 1914 and 1951 of paperweights and bottles in the so-called Whitefriars manner, which raises the question whether this group of types was ever made in the 19th century.

Fortunately, the story of Whitefriars in the 20th century is clearer. Millefiori weights were made from the 1930s until the company closed in 1980. Millefiori paperweights of good collector quality were being made right up to the last day, and they were available to keen searchers in all manner of gift shops, most often at the original prices, for several years thereafter. They have a

This Whitefriars "Partridge in a Pear Tree" weight, which was made in 1979, is of altogether superior merit and unique styling. The degree of complexity in its cane composition is as follows:

		Number of canes
The partridge		300
The date		9
Pears	6 × 200	1,200
Leaves	96 × 80	7,680
Flowers	40 × 7	280
Total		**9,469**

ABOVE
Over the years, Perthshire Paperweights has made a number of hollow-blown weights with various subjects inside, such as ducks and penguins. This example, made in 1988, features a kingfisher.

strong following among collectors. The general cane types made in molds are well formed but fairly simple. The complexity comes in the silhouette designs, in which the subjects are made up of hundreds of tiny, single-color rods, not actually fused together, a technique apparently exclusive to Whitefriars.

Perthshire Paperweights, Scotland, is dedicated to the manufacture of paperweights and related objects. Since 1969 it has produced a large quantity of weights, catering for the gift market and the collector market with clearly differentiated levels of product. Over the years it has produced all traditional patterns of millefiori, and has applied itself successfully in making multicolored silhouettes, using slender rods in the form of a mosaic, the method believed to have been used by the Franchinis in the 19th century.

U.S. MANUFACTURERS

In the United States, the greater preoccupation in the 20th century has been with lampwork and torchwork, although several makers have used millefiori in a subsidiary role. Parabelle Glass is the exception. This company, which was started in 1983 by Gary and Doris Scrutton, has devoted itself exclusively to millefiori, with a very obvious Clichy influence.

ABSTRACTS

Abstract paperweights are a 20th-century phenomenon, just as abstract art is. An abstract paperweight has no regular pattern, and the motif is not representational of a real object, although it may be based on a particular theme. At its most basic, the motif will merely be a haphazard assortment of bubbles or swirling fragments of colored glass, reflecting no obvious skill in the design or making. Such a paperweight will not come within the collector category, although you will encounter these frequently, often purporting to be collectibles. Farther up the scale, motifs will be more contrived and embody a greater skill in the design, shaping, and placing of the motif and its elements. It is the variety of visual effects, which may further be enhanced by faceting and fancy cutting to multiply them, that make abstract paperweights attractive to collectors and makers alike.

BELOW

This modern weight from Kosta, Sweden, features a bubble with a purple trail over a white mushroom.

FAR LEFT

This oddity from Mdina, Malta, is barely in the collector category, although some collectors find the textural patterns in Mdina glass attractive. The shape of this weight perhaps gives it a curiosity value.

Some writers hold that paperweights made using millefiori and lampwork techniques belong to the 19th century, and that in the 20th century glass artists should follow new directions. Certainly abstract glass art gives the artist greater freedom to experiment, and offers greater scope for the exercise of creative talent. Because there is less formality and, in general, fewer processes in their making, they are less labor intensive. They tend, therefore, to be produced in greater quantities, and are less expensive than millefiori or lampworked weights.

In conventional weights, bubbles are usually unintended flaws in the making, but in abstracts bubbles are often an essential part

ABOVE

The U.K. company Langham Glass, Norfolk, made this complicated spiral of green and white ribbons with an air twist in the late 1980s.

ABOVE

"Soothsayer" was made by Selkirk Glass in 1990. This weight, with its silver and gold bubbles and black threads, is typical of the diverse abstract designs in which Peter Holmes specializes.

ABOVE

The intriguing "Space Beacon" by Caithness Glass in 1975 will set you wondering just how that bubble was placed on the peak.

RIGHT

Here is another weight that owes nothing to the 19th century. It was made in 1986 by Correia Art Glass, which was founded in 1974. The exterior is of silver stripes, and the weight has been cut to an unusual shape to reveal the internal iridescent surface.

of the design, sometimes being arranged in patterns, but sometimes being placed as individual and prominent features with skillfully formed shapes. Bubbles can be formed in several ways. The most usual way of creating an individual bubble is to insert a spike into the gather of semi-molten glass, and then to withdraw it. Sometimes a weight will contain many bubbles in a symmetrical pattern, and this will have been made with a jig looking like a bed of nails. The gather of glass is pressed onto the "nails," which leave a pattern of small indentations. Another gather is attached to the first, trapping the air in the indentations.

Swirling shapes of colored glass are made from powdered glass. Sometimes a gather of glass is dipped into, or rolled over, the powder before further working and encasing in another gather of clear class. Sometimes the powder is pushed into the gather with a rotating movement, although this method is typically used to produce gift weights.

A further development is the use of iridescent glass, a technique that was used extensively in the art nouveau period. It involves immersing the glass in a solution of metallic salts or spraying metallic fumes onto the glass during the making or during the cooling period. Iridescence was first used in paperweights in 1972 by two U.S. companies, Lundberg Studios and Orient & Flume.

ABOVE
The U.S. artist Michael O'Keefe
used a pioneering technique to
achieve this fascinating effect with
a motif based on a marine
organism.

ABOVE
Caithness Glass made this beautiful
piece of modern art glass in 1989.
This upright, faceted shape has
become something of a favorite
with this company. This example,
called "Phoenix," was reserved for
members of the Caithness
Collector Club.

In the example below by another U.S. company, Correia Art Glass, the iridescence is coated on an interior surface of the weight. The example by the U.S. artist Michael O'Keefe illustrated here is even more imaginative – it shows a translucent shape, suggestive of a marine organism. The technique used involves melting silver and glass together, and working it at different temperatures to create a variety of colors and degrees of transparency.

The Scottish factories Caithness Glass and Selkirk Glass, although competent in the making of traditional paperweights, have made abstracts their forte. Caithness Glass began producing abstract weights in 1969, the most frequent themes being space/planetary and marine, and the two craftsmen responsible for this initiative were Colin Terris and Peter Holmes. Terris continued to develop new abstract themes at Caithness, expanding it to a fair-sized business, while Holmes left to set up Selkirk Glass in the late 1970s. Caithness paperweights are probably the most extensively marketed of all collector abstracts. A wide selection of limited editions is offered, with quantities of each type ranging from 150 to 750 (some earlier weights were produced in larger quantities). Prices for these modern weights start at around $75 and currently peak at about $300.

LAMPWORK

Lampwork derives its name from the oil-fueled lamp used in the 19th century by glassworkers, who used metal tweezers to manipulate colored glass over a lamp. The lamp has now been replaced by a gas burner or torch, but the word lampwork remains. Colored rods of glass are shaped into a representational subject, which typically consists of several small components, welded together into a fragile assembly. The finished subject is reheated to prevent it from shattering the moment it comes into contact with the molten glass while being encased in clear glass. All the elements of a paperweight with a floral bouquet as its subject – the petals, leaves, tiny stamens, and even the root formations that are sometimes included – are made of glass, and such an assembly is so fragile when it is cold that even the minimum of handling can break it into little pieces.

The magnifying dome overstates the size of the finished weight. When immersed in a bowl of water the refraction is neutralized, showing its real size and revealing the skill that has gone into making the tiny motif.

19TH-CENTURY LAMPWORK

Unlike millefiori, lampwork is not an ancient craft. It is believed to have originated in Venice in the late 16th century, and it was practised in the 17th and 18th centuries. The French, followed by the Belgians and Americans, were the first to apply it to paperweights. As far as is known, the Venetians, Bohemians, and English did not make lampworked paperweights in the 19th century. It is believed that lampwork was practiced to a considerable level of skill in Russia, even though no documentary evidence has yet come to light.

In the 19th century, the most prolific French maker of lampworked weights was Baccarat, followed by St. Louis. Most subjects were floral, although fruit, butterflies, and reptiles were also used. Floral weights tend to be stylized – that is, subjects are symbolic rather than real. A lampworked flower will look "floral" but will make no pretence at being real or even based on a real flower. These stylized flower types are usually given the names of real flowers, not because they resemble the flowers they are named after but because the collecting community has attached those names as a means of recognition.

The Baccarat miniature clematis illustrated here is clearly intended to represent a flower, but by no stretch of the imagination could it be taken for a clematis. Baccarat craftsmen took great care in making what appear at first sight to be simple subjects, and this is a good example. Instead of using a single piece of glass, each petal is shaped with five strips of white glass, lightly coated with pink. The five prominent petals have been overlaid on five lower petals to make a double clematis. The center of the flower is a honeycomb cane – it is white with three concentric rows of hollow, six-pointed, yellow stars. In the center of that cane is a red and white, six-pointed star cane. The leaves are made of white glass, lightly coated with green, but the white base has been shaped so that the coating is of varying intensity, giving an overall veined appearance.

The Baccarat pansy is an example of a semi-stylized flower. The millefiori center and the lower petals of cogged arrow canes make no attempt at realism, but the two large, plum-colored upper petals and the three smaller, lower ones give the overall appearance of a pansy. Notice how the color on the petals is thinner at the edges, so that they are defined by the white almost showing through.

Baccarat pansy

Baccarat dog rose

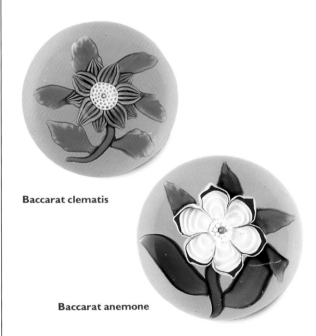

Baccarat clematis

Baccarat anemone

These four 19th-century stylized flowers exhibit the qualities of workmanship and the charm that makes collecting them so addictive.

Combining millefiori with lampwork in floral weights was widely practiced in the 19th century, and all three of the main French factories used millefiori canes as an integral part of the motif, sometimes using a complex cane as the complete flower head, as may be seen in the St. Louis posy shown here. As well as using them in the flowers themselves, Baccarat often surrounded the flower with a single garland of alternate cane types, which finishes off the weight tidily and is typical of the formality running through all Baccarat types. The factory seems to have had a greater sense of orderliness than color, because the garland is often not carefully color-coordinated with the subject, as it would no doubt have been had the Clichy factory used the style.

St. Louis frequently enhanced its floral lampworked weights by mounting the motif on a latticinio basket. The term latticinio, which is derived from the Italian *latte* (milk), refers to the process by which opaque white rods are fused with clear molten glass and rotated to produce a swirling effect. The process is somewhat similar to that described for making filigree canes, but it can be much more complex. St. Louis used latticinio to good effect, and the two paperweights illustrated here show an interesting contrast. In one, the thick, bright white threads set off the luscious fruits and foliage. In the other, the finer threads are a better complement to the finely worked camomile. In this weight, because the flower is white, the latticinio is set upon a pale pink translucent ground to provide a suitable contrast.

Most 19th-century floral motifs are of a single flower. The three main factories did make bouquets, but these are rare and command high prices at auction. The Baccarat and Clichy bouquets reveal the underlying characteristics of these two makers. Baccarat bouquets are always formally presented, with a tidy, symmetrical arrangement. Clichy bouquets, on the other hand, are gathered together in random fashion, as a freshly picked bunch, and often have a piece of ribbon around the stems. Clichy

bouquet weights are the most keenly collected, by those of sufficient means to acquire them, that is.

Most 19th-century lampwork flowers were flat – that is, two-dimensional – probably because three-dimensional work is much more difficult. Three-dimensional flowers usually took the form of an upright bouquet, a type made occasionally by St. Louis and extremely rarely by Baccarat. Those produced by St. Louis usually had a torsade around the base, and they were not always successful. The main problems lay in making a well-formed, symmetrical bouquet and in centering it accurately in the weight. Both factories cut this type of weight with facets. Sometimes large, concave facets were used, but the best results were achieved with multi-honeycomb facets over the upper part of the dome, as shown in the example here.

Floral weights made in the United States in the 19th century have a strong collector following, and they are not without merit, but in general they fall somewhat short of their French counterparts. The two most important factories producing floral lampwork were the New England Glass Company (N.E.G.C.) and the Boston & Sandwich Glass Company. The N.E.G.C. bouquet illustrated on page 43 is of exceptional quality.

For a number years some superb lampworked floral plaques and paperweights with flowers in the same style were believed to have been made by the Mount Washington Glass Co. In 1978 the

ABOVE
This floral plaque, possibly Russian and dating from *c.*1880, is of a type that used to be attributed to the U.S. Mount Washington Glass Co. The exact origin of this fine plaque is still unknown, and only five plaques of this type are known to exist. (Photograph courtesy the Corning Museum of Glass)

paperweight historian, Paul Hollister, suggested that these were of Russian origin, a view that was reinforced in 1990, when Dwight P. Lanmon, director of the Corning Museum of Glass, found supporting evidence in Russian museums. Since then further examples of lampwork from eastern Europe have come to light. However, although the distinctive floral plaques and weights are now known not to have been of U.S. manufacture, it is almost certain that they will continue to be known as Mount Washington weights. They are fine examples of the lampworker's craft – they are unusually realistic for the 19th century, and certainly as good as any work produced by the French.

For practical purposes, we should assume that of the main French factories, only Baccarat and St. Louis made fruit weights. From time to time, fruit weights of unprovable origin have been attributed to Clichy and to Pantin, but this has not been confirmed. The format of the St. Louis fruit illustrated on page 41 is quite common – an apple, two pears, and a few cherries set on a bed of leaves, all on a latticinio basket – and this formula produces an attractive presentation that will stand out well in any display. St. Louis also produced fruits singly and in pairs, as well as some rather odd turnip weights. The example illustrated is by far the most successful, but it is comparatively common so tends to be less expensive than the other types. A few examples of St. Louis strawberries consist of a single fruit with a flower.

The only fruit that can be attributed with reasonable certainty to Baccarat is the strawberry. This usually consists of one ripe and one unripe fruit with its associated foliage.

When it comes to butterfly weights, Baccarat provides the classic 19th-century example. It is stylized, and it consists almost entirely of millefiori canes. The wings are cross sections of a marbled cane type used exclusively for this purpose, and the body is a tube of purple gauze. The eyes are small blue chips set in the head, and the body is completed with two black antennae. Baccarat sometimes set a large butterfly within a circular garland of canes; sometimes a slightly smaller butterfly hovers over a flower. The butterfly and flower weights are generally the most highly regarded, but the quality can be very variable. At their best they are magnificent, but they can be spoiled by an indifferent flower with poor foliage.

Baccarat also seems to have had difficulty in getting the butterfly right, because most are flawed. Typical faults are detached or broken antennae, distorted wings, and indistinct or out-of-position eyes. Collectors intent on having one of these weights must tolerate some imperfection in assembled quality.

The snake weights made by Baccarat and St. Louis are not always regarded favorably by collectors, but they are extremely rare and carry a much higher price than is justified by their intrinsic merit.

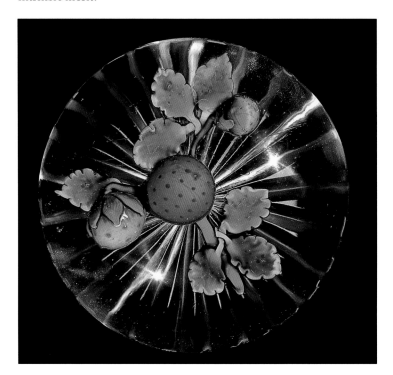

ABOVE
Paul Stankard's "Sippewisset Bouquet" was made in 1979 and was representative of his best work at that time. It combines the best elements of artistic composition with the finest attention to detail, and established a standard few have been able to equal.

20TH-CENTURY LAMPWORK

During the 20th century, lampwork has taken different directions in Europe and in the United States.

In Europe, paperweights have been made in glass factories. Paul Ysart, for example, the leading pioneer in the 1930s, was a glassworker first, operating in factories whose primary output was other products. The same is true of subsequent makers, with the sole exception of the Scottish factory Perthshire Paperweights Ltd., which was founded in 1968 and dedicated to paperweight manufacture. The fine French crystal manufacturers Baccarat and St. Louis, although producing paperweights with obvious enthusiasm, also made a wide range of other articles.

In Europe, therefore, paperweights were made in an environment of established glass-craft skills, backed by a fine tradition, and by the best available equipment, particularly the furnaces and glass tanks. The weights were made in the traditional manner, with the factories making their own glass, melting it, and using it in its liquid form.

In the United States, on the other hand, glass artists of the paperweight renaissance, starting with Charles Kaziun, worked singly and in a small studio, without the conventional factory equipment. Although the processes involved in making the lampworked subjects at the bench with a gas torch were the same as in a factory, the encapsulation process was different. Studio artists do not make their own glass – they buy optical quality "slugs" of glass, which they heat at the bench with a torch. This glass contains no lead, but is very clear and is less susceptible to striations (visible lines in the glass caused during its rotation in working). Each part of the assembly – the stamens in a flower and sometimes the flower head itself, for example – is encased in a protective "module" of glass. The module is further encased with the rest of the motif. The final product consists of a base, the motif and its modules, and the crown, and at no stage is liquid glass used. When such a weight is held up to the light, the join of the base to the crown and the outline of the little protective modules around the most delicate parts are visible.

Purists may claim that such paperweights are not the real thing, but this way of working enables an artist to work singly and to start up without the large capital expenditure of a fully fledged glassworks. It is, therefore, a less expensive option. It also gives the artist greater flexibility, and eliminates the problems of flaws and distortion that have to be overcome when liquid glass is used. Perthshire Paperweights, for example, has claimed a reject rate of some 70 percent for collector weights. Some established artists now use small furnaces to heat the glass slugs, because it is faster, more efficient, and results in a better weld. In these cases the joins are less visible.

To achieve economies of scale, European makers of lampworked weights for the collectors' market produced them in series of between 150 and 300. For the same reason studio artists are obliged to make their designs in series, but they tend to limit the quantities they produce to 25–75 for each design.

As in millefiori, European makers initially followed the styles and patterns of their 19th-century predecessors. As they gained experience, they developed their own designs. St. Louis made a number of virtual copies of well-known antique weights, including a date-cane to avoid confusion. The date-cane is integral in the design, and is often so unobtrusive that it can be found only by keen searching. In most cases, modern versions of antique weights do not compare favorably with the originals, even though better glass that is free from distortions and impurities is used. The St. Louis bouquet shown below replicates the antique style, while not actually copying a particular weight. In this case the modern craftsmen have produced a flawless example of a technically

ABOVE
This finely executed fruit weight, made by Ray Banford in 1981, was inspired by one of the finest ever made – a 19th-century example with two large pears against filigree canes, variously attributed to Clichy and Pantin, and now in the Bergstrom-Mahler Museum.

LEFT
The upright bouquet of rich green foliage by St. Louis is packed with flowers, it is perfectly centered and it stands upright within its evenly applied double overlay. The *SL1983* signature-cane is one of the flower centers.

ABOVE
This water lily, made in 1977, is one of Baccarat's finest modern pieces. The white petals of the flower are beautifully shaped, the stamens stand firmly in position, and the whole floats on a dark green, viscous pond.

BELOW RIGHT
This unique subject, "Escargot," was made by Baccarat in 1977. On a stony ground with a few flowers, this predates the American environmental weights made from 1984 onwards, but it was perhaps itself influenced by the Pantin salamander weights made c.1878.

FAR RIGHT
As well as its lovely coloring, this artistic composition, depicting a kingfisher perched among the reeds, has several delightful touches. The green leaves are folded over and shaded to make them look three-dimensional; the little white canes form the simple florets; and the wings of the bird, which are not lampworked, are an assembly of canes effectively simulating the feathers. It was made in 1989.

difficult subject, which, were it an antique, would be extremely expensive.

This paperweight is an example of a double overlay, so called because the weight has been overlaid with a covering of red glass on white (the white makes the red opaque). Finally, "window" facets, called "printies" or "punties" by collectors, are cut so that the interior motif may be seen. Part of the attraction of collecting modern weights is to watch each year for new editions of the principal factories, and to spot examples of exceptional quality such as this.

Baccarat made a more significant departure from 19th-century styling. According to its own literature, its modern lampwork dates from 1968, but it acknowledges that saleable quality came later. It was from *c.* 1976 that the company began to produce collector lampworked weights of considerable quality and originality. Baccarat acknowledges the help of the U.S. artist Francis D. Whittemore in developing its lampwork techniques, but has certainly gone on to establish its own style with bold subjects in semi- and fully three-dimensional form. The three examples illustrated – a snail, water lily, and kingfisher – show a departure from convention in overall design and in detailed composition. They reflect the consistently superb quality seen in most Baccarat 20th-century weights. They are always full-sized, about 3¼ inches in diameter, and they have a generous dome, are made of high quality crystal, and, as a paperweight should, feel heavy.

These four weights by Paul Ysart show just a fraction of his considerable repertoire and skill. Unlike other artists who make collectible weights, Ysart had no expert help – he was the pioneer, and the quality of his work is the more remarkable for that. The triple insect, which uses aventurine, was made in the 1950s; the other three weights were made in the 1970s.

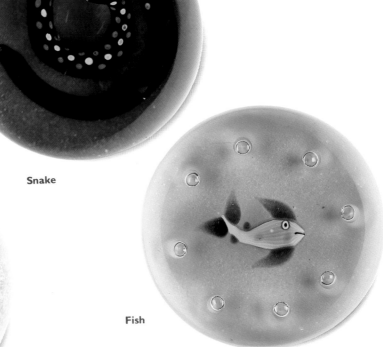

Snake

Stylized flower

Triple insect

Fish

Paul Ysart, the founder of paperweight-making in Scotland, developed a formidable talent for most aspects of the paperweight art, and his lampworked weights are keenly sought by collectors. The four different types illustrated here represent the range of his work. He often used aventurine, colored glass impregnated with particles of copper to give it a sparkling appearance, which was first used in paperweights by the Venetians in the 19th century. Ysart's best weights are signed with either a *PY* or an *H* cane, the difference being due to a marketing agreement which restricted the *PY* signature to those sold in the United States.

William Manson, who was trained by Ysart at Caithness Glass, has produced many fine weights both for Caithness Glass and under his own name. The three-dimensional rosebud on a sand ground shown on page 49 was made for Caithness in 1979. Manson's range is very broad, and some of his best work has been in marine subjects, such as fish and stingrays. Manson often uses aventurine in his weights.

John Deacons is another talented Scot. Formerly with Perthshire Paperweights, he has marketed his products under the name of J. Glass, S.T.K. and John Deacons. Most of his work is floral and in the traditional French style. The flower illustrated on page 49,

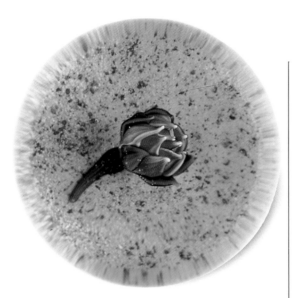

ABOVE
There is a touch of pathos about this rosebud – it has been cut from the rose but left forgotten on the sand. The weight was made by William Manson in 1979, just before he left Caithness Glass to set up on his own.

ABOVE
The 1978 series of 250 "butterfly on a flower" weights by Caithness Glass was oversubscribed by collectors, and it was repeated in 1979. In this 1978 version the butterfly is made of translucent aventurine. The lampwork was by William Manson.

for example, is a virtual copy of an antique Baccarat type, but the motif is enhanced by being mounted on a cushion, made crown fashion from filigree canes, a device sometimes also used by Ysart. This weight is signed with a date-cane, *JD*.

Perthshire Paperweights of Scotland began to make simple lampworked weights in 1970. These were similar in style to some basic 19th-century types, and the late Stuart Drysdale, then head of the company, acknowledged the debt owed to the 19th-century masters, whom he tried to emulate but not copy. Over the years the lampwork subjects of Perthshire weights have become increasingly sophisticated, but their merit more often lies in the enhancement techniques rather than in the lampwork itself. The company has produced numerous overlays with conventional and unusual cutting, and latticinio that is equal in fineness and precision to that made by St. Louis in the 19th century. Its crowning achievement has been with encased overlays, however.

An encased overlay is a weight that has first been overlaid, usually with a color over white, cut with facets, and then further encased in a layer of clear glass. This technique requires considerable craft skill, and has a very high spoilage rate. In the 19th century, only St. Louis and Bacchus attempted the process; in the 20th century, only Perthshire and St. Louis have risen to the challenge. Perthshire encased overlays are produced as one-of-a-kind weights, and a few have been taken to a more advanced stage in the form of a double overlay encased with a double overlay. No

ABOVE
This stylized flower was made by John Deacons in 1991.

ABOVE
This bright little example from Perthshire Paperweights features a basket of green canes drawn underneath to enclose the flower and take the place of a ground. It was made in 1978.

FAR LEFT
Chris Buzzini had worked for Orient & Flume, Lundberg Studios, and Correia Art Glass before beginning to make paperweights in his own right in 1987. As this bright orange flower suggests, his work has a look of Stankard about it.

LEFT
Ken Rosenfeld began making paperweights in 1984. This bright red and yellow bouquet, made in 1990, is one of his more colorful offerings.

other manufacturer has yet matched this, possibly because it is not commercially viable.

The weights made by studio artists in the United States are, as a rule, easily distinguished from those made in Europe, the use of optical quality glass giving a particularly limpid appearance. U.S. makers tend to be somewhat more economic in their use of glass, as few make weights as large as, say, Baccarat, and several have a flattish profile. The styling, too, is very different, and it is appropriate to reflect on how this has developed.

Charles Kaziun, the pioneer of the studio artist movement, began with glass buttons, moving on to their larger cousins in the early 1940s. He was fascinated by the crimped roses made by the Whitall Tatum company at the beginning of the century, and eventually he found a way of producing roses and tulips in the same manner, and of equal, if not superior, quality. He incorporated these in paperweights, and also in decorative bottles and decanters. Kaziun went on to produce lampworked weights of great precision, sometimes using a traditional 19th-century motif such as a stylized pansy, and sometimes introducing his own design, such as a miniature lily. In all cases, his weights had an elegant simplicity.

Years later other artists began to follow his example – Francis Whittemore in 1968, Paul Stankard in 1969, father and son Ray and Bob Banford in 1971, for example. Thereafter a succession of new artists, most from a background of glass, typically scientific glasswork, made simple, stylized, flat floral weights. Throughout the 1970s and 1980s, the work of the U.S. studio artists was characterized by increasing attention to detail, and a greater precision in the working, which was made possible by the method of encapsulation.

ABOVE
Bob Banford and his father Ray began to make paperweights in 1971. Bob's main output is of stylized floral subjects with high quality, accurate working. This weight was made in 1993.

In 1975 Paul Stankard began a series of orchid studies. This example, of which 75 were made in 1977, is rated as one of his most serious, being a faithful reproduction of the spider orchid *Brassia caudata,* right down to the tiny marks on the tendrils.

Gradually, however, new ground was broken, and from around 1972, almost imperceptibly, Paul Stankard began to introduce greater reality into his subjects. He selected rather unusual botanical species, and reproduced the detailed elements in glass, including the stamens in the flower heads and the roots. By the late 1970s, his work was such that he was regarded by some as the finest paperweight lampwork artist of either the 19th or the 20th century. His spider orchid, shown above, is typical of the botanical accuracy he achieved. Stankard has continued to develop new techniques and approaches.

He created three-dimensional effects by making compound weights – that is, with elements of the subject on different layers of f glass – and moved to fully three-dimensional studies by making weights of upright, rectangular shape, showing the full plant including the roots, and placing among them fanciful humanoid figures. He has enhanced several of these studies, which he called "cloistered botanicals," by having them laminated on three sides with coloured translucent glass. Although they will be beyond the reach of all but the wealthiest of collectors – at the time of writing a price of $15,000 is typical – they rank among the truly great works in glass artistry of the 20th century.

In 1978, Rick Ayotte, encouraged by Stankard, began to make bird subjects. He aimed for reality from the outset, and within a few years he was reproducing in glass not only the features of defined bird types, but also the textures of feathers and so on. Perhaps his finest works to date are his three-dimensional bird landscapes, the first of which was completed in 1986. Having

ABOVE

This spectacular weight from Rick Ayotte is more than just a butterfly. The quest for accuracy is evident.

ABOVE

Rick Ayotte's miniature blue tit, made in 1984, displays the ornithological accuracy for which he has become well known. His weights tend to have a flattish profile, which may be intended to diminish the magnifying effect of the dome.

ABOVE
This 1983 weight is the result of collaboration between three artists – Debbie Tarsitano made the floral bouquet, her father, Delmo, made the realistic-looking spider, and Max Erlacher engraved the web and dragonfly trapped in it on the base.

ABOVE
Victor Trabucco started to make paperweights in 1977, and he has since established a reputation for highly artistic creations, often in unconventional formats. He was the first artist to find a way of eliminating the tell-tale dividing line that was a characteristic of U.S. weights. This yellow rose, which dates from 1989, is one of his conventional pieces.

perfected his technique with birds, Ayotte has branched out into the more conventional areas of floral and butterfly subjects, again aiming for reality with defined species.

The traditional lampwork format of a single subject, such as a flower or bouquet, continued to predominate, but around 1984 another studio artist, Delmo Tarsitano, began to produce what he called an "earth life" series of weights with spiders, reptiles, and so on in natural surroundings. At about the same time, Stankard introduced his "environmental" series, which featured botanical subjects growing in the soil. These were the forerunners of the Ayotte "birdscapes" of a couple of years later, and they are typical of the ways in which some artists continually strive to break free of the conventional mold. In 1983, Debbie Tarsitano collaborated with the engraver Max Erlacher to produce some weights with an engraving on the base that complemented the encased floral motif. The bouquet, spider (by Delmo), and web, illustrated left, is an interesting example of that period.

Victor Trabucco began making paperweights in 1977. He had for some years created glass sculptures, and when he came to make paperweights he did not confine himself to the conventional spherical format. Some of his work appears in irregular faceted shapes – which he has called "Nature in Ice" – and some in impressive magnums.

TORCHWORK

A major departure from tradition in glass art has been the development of torchwork as an alternative to lampwork. Rods of colored glass are heated, shaped, and trailed onto the surface of a gather of semi-molten glass taken from a furnace. This is covered with a layer of clear glass. The process can be repeated to produce three-dimensional effects. Lundberg Studios and Orient & Flume have used this technique imaginatively and with great success.

LEFT
It is surprising that marine themes were not used more in the past, because glass seems to be the perfect medium for the subject. Torchwork, applied in successive layers, is an ideal technique for the purpose, and has been used by Orient & Flume in this 1988 example.

·························· DUMPS ··························

Anyone who browses in British antique shops and fairs is sure to have come across the green glass objects known as dumps, thousands of which were made over a long period. Although these are not really paperweights, they are, by convention, classified with them, and, as they are now very collectible, they are included here.

They were first made in the 19th century from green bottle glass, and it is thought that they were made at the end of the day from glass that would otherwise have been dumped – hence the name. They are also referred to as "doorstops," which is a more practical and appropriate description. They are fairly crude pieces, requiring only the basic skills of the glassmaker, but several processes are involved in their manufacture, and they do have a certain attraction. There are four main kinds.

The flower pot consists of a crudely formed pot with an upright flower emerging from it. The flower head and stem will often be made of a bubble, shaped for the purpose. The pot and flower petals will have a chalky, transparent appearance, and they were probably made by sprinkling powdered chalk over semi-molten glass and then covering it with another layer of glass. Sometimes the flower is single, but some taller versions have two or three layers of petals rising above each other.

ABOVE
This is a three-tiered version of the flower pot, a common type of 19th-century dump.

LEFT
This single flower pot dump is impressed on the base *J. Kilner Maker*, dating it fairly accurately *c.*1829.

LEFT
This 19th-century dump weight, packed with bubbles, is one of the most common types of dump.

ABOVE
Ceres, the Roman goddess of agriculture, is represented on the sulfide in this 19th-century dump.

The second kind has the same design and shape as the flower pot, but the petals appear to be made of silver foil, which some collectors find more attractive.

The third kind is packed with tear-shaped bubbles, which give the appearance of a mass of falling raindrops, while the fourth contains a sulfide – a china clay figure, of a variety of subjects, but always crudely formed. These sulfides are greatly inferior to sulfides proper, which are described later.

Apart from those that bear a maker's stamp, the bases of 19th-century dumps are jagged, where the glass has been broken away from the pontil rod and not ground smoothly away.

There is no documentary record of the history of green glass dumps, but because some were stamped on the base by their makers, they can be dated reasonably accurately. The first dumps were probably made in 1829 by two firms, John Kilner and J. Tower. Kilner dumps have four different stamps on the base, and the historical records of the company place them in this chronological order: J. Kilner, Maker; J. Kilner, Maker, Wakefield; J. Kilner & Son; and J. Kilner & Sons. In 1844 the company became Kilner Brothers.

Dumps continued to be made into the 20th century, probably until bottle-making became mechanized. They are now sought after by collectors, and it is quite possible that many have been made recently, especially as they require no more than basic glassmaking skills. The collector should therefore be alert when paying $150 or more for these so-called antiques.

ABOVE
This is a good example of the rarer, silver flower 19th-century dump weight.

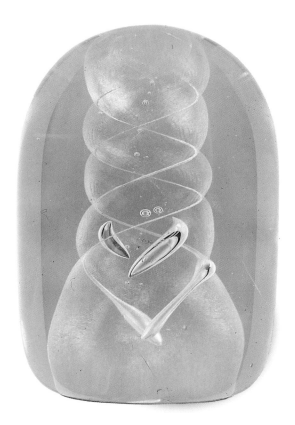

This 20th-century dump weight is very rare. It was made in 1983 by Midsummer Glass, a small company in Cambridge, U.K., which was forced to close a few years later. Its main business was the production of art glass, and it made only a few paperweights of this type. The use of iridescence is unusual, and the effect was created by blowing metallic fumes onto a gather of semi-molten glass that had been twisted into the shape seen here, which was then encased in clear glass.

ABOVE
This dump was made by Hartley Wood in 1993. The company offers the opportunity to have a dump that is in pristine condition, unravaged by the harsh treatment that 19th-century examples have invariably suffered.

In 1992, the British glassmaker Hartley Wood & Co. Ltd. began to make dumps in the Victorian style. They cost $45–$60, and are available by mail order (see left). There is no danger that these will be mistaken for antiques – the glass is a better quality, and the base is ground flat to remove the pontil mark so that they can be used as paperweights without scratching the desk.

Victorian dumps will often show their age. They will generally not have been so well cared for as paperweights, and because of their comparatively low value, they are not worth the cost of restoration to remove scratches and bruises.

At the time of writing, asking prices will vary from around $100 for a simple bubble type to approximately $250 for a good example of the flower type with a maker's stamp.

·····························SULFIDES·····························

A sulfide is a china clay cameo encased in clear glass, and paperweights were just one of several media to exploit the technique.

The subjects were usually the heads of historically important people, and even before they were used in paperweights they had been included in plaques, medallions, scent bottles, and other miscellaneous glass articles.

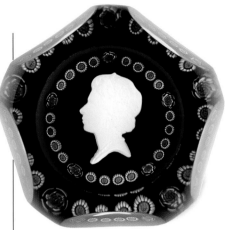

ABOVE
Baccarat made this weight to commemorate the jubilee anniversary of Queen Elizabeth II. It was sculpted by Gilbert Poillerat and made in an edition of 500.

ABOVE
This sulfide was made by Selkirk Glass in the late 1970s to celebrate the 80th birthday of Queen Elizabeth, The Queen Mother.

ABOVE
Because most sulfides were contained in articles other than paperweights, a couple of examples are shown here. They are collected as "paperweight-related articles," and appear at auction as such. This fine scent bottle featuring William Shakespeare by Apsley Pellatt would fetch around $750 at auction.

ABOVE
This sulfide weight by Apsley Pellatt pictures the Duke of Wellington.

ABOVE
St. Louis made this sulfide of Pope John Paul II in a white overlay in 1981.

The first experiments in encasing china clay in glass are believed to have taken place in the mid-18th century. The process was difficult, partly because the different rates of contraction of the cameo and the glass during cooling led to distortion and cracking. In 1818, a successful process was patented by Pierre Honoré Boudon de Saint-Amans in France. In the following year, an improved and different process was patented by Apsley Pellatt in Britain. This process inserted the preheated cameo into an envelope of glass, then collapsed the envelope, using the dangerous sounding method of sucking out the air through the glassblower's tube.

It is likely that sulfide paperweights were first made in the 1840s together with the millefiori and lampworked weights, and,

ABOVE
A 19th-century patch box by Baccarat is decorated with a sulfide of the Duc de Bordeaux.

in fact, some combine millefiori canes with a sulfide.

The cameo is produced from a mold, which was made from an original sculpture specifically for the purpose. When they are encased in glass, 19th-century, sulfides often take on an attractive, silvery appearance, and the glass seems to highlight the detailed features, giving them an altogether improved perspective. The paperweight revival of the early 1950s began with sulfides at both Baccarat and St. Louis in France. A third French factory, Cristalleries D'Albret, has also made sulfides, but although some manufacture has taken place on a minor scale elsewhere, only French manufacturers have produced significant quantities.

Sulfides occupy a relatively minor role in paperweight collecting, and perhaps for that reason they tend not to be so highly priced either as antiques or as new products. This is in contrast to the 18th and 19th centuries, when they are said to have commanded substantial prices, probably because of the great technical difficulties in making them.

############## M ISCELLANEOUS T YPES ##############

SWIRLS

A swirl looks like a pinwheel. In the 19th century, swirls were made in much the same way as latticinio, but the alternate opaque white and colored rods are thicker and there is less clear glass between them. Because the central junction would otherwise look unsightly, it is topped with a feature cane.

In the 19th century, Clichy made swirls. Although similar weights were produced by Bohemian glassmakers, the opaque rods do not swirl — they are more upright — and they are usually referred to as crowns. Clichy swirls are set low in the weight to secure the best effect from magnification, and the usual colors are various shades of blue with white, and pink with white. A two-color swirl is more highly valued, and a swirl with a Clichy rose at the center carries a very high price.

In the 20th century, French and Scottish makers have produced swirls that appear to have been manufactured in a similar fashion, although not always in the Clichy manner, and the three modern examples illustrated here and on the next page, together with the original Clichy version, show some interesting contrasts.

The St. Louis pink and white miniature is an outstanding example of modern glass-making. The swirl is perfectly formed,

ABOVE
This good, tidy example of a swirl was made by Clichy c.1850. Clichy swirls can bend in either direction, and therefore cannot be used for identification purposes.

ABOVE
From a distance, most collectors would identify this as a Clichy weight. The central cane, however, would point them towards a Scottish maker, and it was, in fact, made by John Deacons in the early 1980s. At the time, Deacons was producing large quantities of these weights, testifying either to their ease of manufacture or to his personal skills. This example was bought in the 1980s in a local shop for $12.

appearing as a hollow ball and filling the weight, which is neatly topped by the St. Louis version of a Clichy rose. This is cream-colored with a tiny red rose at the center, the whole combining to make a charming little weight.

MARBRIES

Antique marbries were created by St. Louis. The name derives from the French *marbre* (marble), but it is only by some stretch of the imagination that the type could be said to have a marbled appearance. The surface of the weight seems to be patterned and encased in a fine skin of clear glass. The pattern consists of colored festoons draped in four segments of the sphere against a white background, and sometimes more than one color was used.

Antique examples were hollow-blown, and they were made by trailing strips of semi-molten glass over a ball of white glass, with further working to ensure that the color was flush with the base. They are exceptionally rare, and sell for high prices on the few occasions they come to the salerooms. In June 1992, a good blue and white example was sold in London for $9,200.

Modern versions are not common either, but are less expensive. Orient & Flume made a marbrie in the late 1970s, and St. Louis made a two-color example in 1971. Selkirk Glass made two

ABOVE
**Orient & Flume made this
iridescent weight in 1979. It was
hand-engraved by L. Richer to
show an elk, pheasant, and hawk
among trees and grasses.**

RIGHT
**George Thiewes made these three
small, surface-patterned weights in
the early 1980s. Each has an
entirely different design, but they
share the same high quality.**

ABOVE
**This iridescent weight, with a motif
of peacock feathers, was made by
Okra Glass in the mid-1980s. This
is, in fact, a common expression of
iridescence, and the type was also
produced by both Lundberg
Studios and Orient & Flume, the
output of each being difficult to
distinguish.**

versions in 1980 – one pink on white, and the other with white trails on a dark blue globe. The Selkirk models sold in 1980 for just $46, an incredibly low price for such a fine piece of craftsmanship.

SURFACE-PATTERNED WEIGHTS

If the few externally painted weights of unknown manufacture dating from the 19th century are excluded, these are a 20th-century development. The most common are those using iridescent glass, reminiscent of the art nouveau period and the works of Tiffany and Loetz.

The earliest examples of iridescent glass were Roman, but the process is the result of centuries of exposure to metallic oxides in the earth, which corrode the glass, giving it a shimmering effect. In the late 19th century, European glassmakers began to create iridescent glass by immersing it in a solution of metallic salts, or by exposing the hot glass to chemical fumes. The American Louis Comfort Tiffany produced the most striking results, establishing a

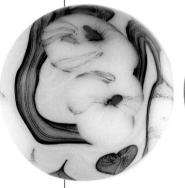

fashion in art glass that continues today. Tiffany made few paperweights, however, and the surface-patterned iridescent type first emerged in 1972 from the factories of Lundberg Studios and Orient & Flume in California.

In Britain, Okra, a Birmingham-based company, has been producing iridescent weights of various designs for many years; these tend to be at the lower end of the collector price range.

The surface-patterned weights made by George Thiewes are something of a modern rarity. His work was not promoted extensively, and he appears to have made weights of exceptional quality for a short period in the late 1970s and early 1980s. As a type these attractive little weights are unique, and it is surprising that others have not taken up the techniques for producing them.

A 19th-century pinchbeck weight depicting a rural scene.

This 19th-century picture weight has a portrait of the young Queen Victoria.

This engraved Indian head is by Max Erlacher, the well-known U.S. engraver.

PINCHBECK WEIGHTS

Pinchbeck weights are named after Christopher Pinchbeck (1670–1732), the inventor of an alloy used as a substitute for gold in jewelry. These weights consist of a base with a scene in metallic relief attached to a glass dome. The metallic leaf is mounted onto marble or pewter, which is glued or screwed to the glass dome. Some of the scenes are very finely worked, and this is an unusual area of collecting, which can be quite rewarding.

It is believed that pinchbeck weights were popular *c*. 1850. There is no possibility that Christopher Pinchbeck himself was involved in their production, and the country or countries of origin are unknown. At the time of writing, a good example will sell for about £350 (approximately $525) in London.

PICTURE WEIGHTS

These are not really in the mainstream of paperweight collecting, as they are simply pictures or trade advertisements stuck underneath a clear glass block. They have no technical merit, but some have historical interest, as the first ones appeared in the mid-19th century.

ENGRAVED WEIGHTS

Although engraved weights are decorative, they are not, in general, keenly collected. There are exceptions, however, when the quality of the engraving is exceptionally good, as in the Indian head by Max Erlacher shown to the left.

CHAPTER THREE

IDENTIFYING PAPERWEIGHTS

A ttribution is part of the fun of collecting, and all collectors are keen to develop their skills in this area. Although it might be argued that it is somewhat academic to speculate on whether a weight was made in one factory or another, collectors do like to know what they have and where it was made – they like to be able to recognize a product for what it is, as well as to appreciate its qualities. There is also the question of value, for whether a weight is of 19th- or 20th-century origin has some bearing on the price.

One of the first questions a non-collector will ask is, "How can you tell an antique from a modern weight?" This question is difficult to answer because there is no single method, the basis of identification being the knowledge and experience accumulated over a long period and from contact with a variety of different kinds of weight. It is not within the scope of this book to provide a comprehensive basis for identification. There are books specifically dedicated to that purpose, such as the two excellent works on 19th-century weights by George N. Kulles. It is, however, appropriate to consider the important factors and the various methods used, and to give a few tips.

A B O V E

The strawberry has proved difficult to reproduce realistically in glass, but Delmo Tarsitano succeeded in this 1983 weight. The flowers and foliage may seem very artificial, but the fruit itself is excellent.

CANES

The canes are the most obvious method of identifying millefiori weights. Collectors will fairly quickly learn to recognize the 19th-century cane types of Baccarat, St. Louis, Clichy, and Bohemia by comparing actual examples and photographs. The direction of spiral twists will also provide a clue for French makers. Baccarat spiral canes slope up to the left when viewed horizontally. St. Louis and Clichy canes slope up to the right.

The photographs in this book will serve as a good identification reference. There has as yet been no comprehensive pictorial reference on modern millefiori canes, and several illustrations are provided here in order to back up the general photography for identification purposes.

ABOVE
20th-century Baccarat.

ABOVE
Selkirk Glass, Scotland.

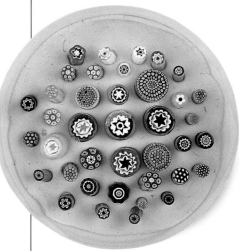

ABOVE
20th-century Vasart Glass, Scotland.

ABOVE
Perthshire Paperweights, Scotland.

RIGHT
20th-century Whitefriars, UK.

ABOVE
Made by Parabelle Glass, U.S.A., in the 20th century.

ABOVE
These 20th-century Moretti cane set-ups from Murano would be appropriate for jewelry.

ABOVE
20th-century Cape Cod, U.S.A.

ABOVE
20th century Paul Ysart.

LEFT
20th-century Murano.

Canes do not, however, provide conclusive evidence of the manufacturer's identity, for they can find their way into the hands of those who incorporate them into their own products. A few years ago, fake Paul Ysart weights appeared on the market with *PY* canes that were probably original.

Canes should not be used alone in the identification of 19th-century U.S. weights. Migrant craftsmen from Europe played a significant role in paperweight making, and it is believed that some took canes from their former employees with them. Nicholas Lutz, for example, was apprenticed at St. Louis from 1845 and joined the Boston & Sandwich Glass Co. in 1869. William Gillinder learned his paperweight skills at Bacchus & Co., Birmingham, England, and the weights subsequently produced at his Philadelphia company bear so striking a resemblance to those made by Bacchus that even experts can have difficulty in identifying them. Other clues to makers are provided by:

- Cane patterns and their methods of grouping
- Basic types of weight
- Detailed characteristics of the lampwork
- Type and style of lampworked subject
- Type of ground used
- Colors
- Faceting characteristics (although some weights have been recut as part of restoration)

These are all visual means of identification. Some limited work has been done in identifying weight makers through the specific gravity of the glass, but more popular has been the process of fluorescence testing, which involves exposing the weight to ultraviolet light in a darkened room. The fluorescent color emitted has nothing to do with the perceived colors in the weight; it is caused by the chemical composition of the glass. Some reasonably consistent results have been obtained using this method, although it is as well to bear in mind Paul Ysart's view that the sources of basic materials and the resulting composition of the glass varied from batch to batch.

······················· PROFILES ·······················

The profile of a weight – that is, its shape when viewed from the side – is often stated as one basis for identification. Experience, however, will prove it to be of little value. Almost all 19th-century weights available to collectors have been restored. Minor restoration is sometimes called polishing, but whatever the term, it means that a layer of glass has been ground away to remove offending scratches, chips or bruises. If the damage is light, the reduction of glass will be minimal, but in most cases a significant amount will have been ground away, in one exercise or, more likely, a succession of them. The diagrams here show examples of actual weights from the three main French factories. The larger outlines are not themselves the full size because they have been restored, while it is clear that the smaller versions have suffered rather more than polishing to bring them to their reduced state. You should use the larger profiles shown to judge the extent of any restoration that may have taken place. The greater the reduction, the lower must be the price!

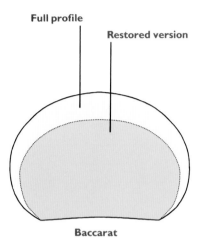

Full profile

Restored version

Baccarat

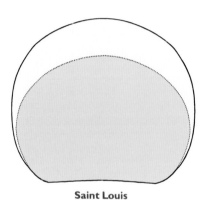

Saint Louis

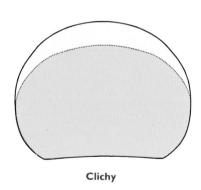

Clichy

ABOVE
Baccarat, Saint Louis, and Clichy paperweight profiles. The darker blue shading indicates their profiles after restoration.

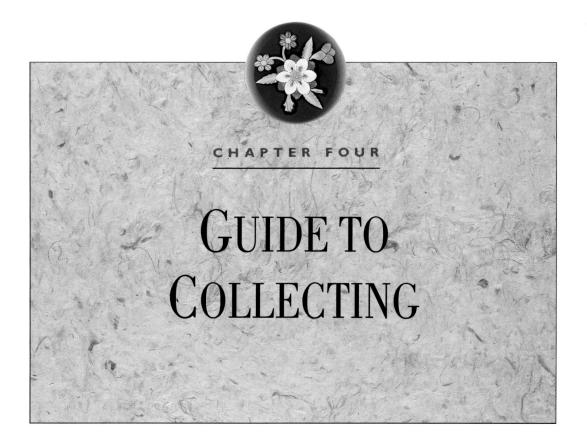

CHAPTER FOUR

GUIDE TO COLLECTING

Many collectors start with an inexpensive purchase, and become fascinated with the form, which leads them to make further acquisitions. Eventually, as they become familiar with what is available, they begin to regret their earlier lack of knowledge and some of the early purchases.

Apart from understanding the scope of paperweights and where they are made, there are many other ways in which the satisfaction derived from forming a collection may be enhanced – knowing how they are made, understanding the historical background and the latest research in this area, learning how to identify the products of the various makers, seeing important collections, discovering about the artists and new talents, knowing what is coming to auction, and following the price trends are just a few. To get the most out of collecting paperweights, you will need a good understanding of the whole subject.

·························· L I T E R A T U R E ··························

The first and most obvious path is the existing literature on the subject, and many useful books are listed in Further Reading on page 78. The most scholarly book on paperweights is Paul

ABOVE

This Clichy bouquet, dating from c.1850, is, with its triangular arrangement, a little more formal than is usual for this type, but it displays all that factory's quality. The ribbon around the stems was, in the nineteenth century, found only on Clichy bouquets.

LEFT

Paul Stankard has established a reputation that reaches outside the ranks of paperweight collectors. In 1992, the Corning Museum of Glass chose this 1987 example to exhibit at the Yokohama Museum of Art, Japan, in its Masterpieces of Glass from the Corning Museum exhibition. The subject, "Indian Pipe," exemplifies the artist's preoccupation with unusual botanical studies, showing ghostly flowers rising from a secret world beneath the earth, to which the viewer is invited. The strange humanoid figures are Stankard's "spirits under the earth." (Photograph courtesy the Corning Museum of Glass)

ABOVE

The few surviving examples of the outstanding Mount Washington rose present something of a mystery. Although they have been attributed to the Mount Washington Glass Co., there is little evidence of paperweight making at that factory. To the art lover and collector, concerned more with intrinsic merit than provenance, the question is immaterial, for these are truly remarkable works. (Photograph courtesy the Corning Museum of Glass)

Hollister's *The Encyclopedia of Glass Paperweights*, which was the first comprehensive study of the subject. It is a primary reference book for all collectors. More up-to-date reference, including information on studio artists, is contained in Lawrence H. Selman's *The Art of the Paperweight*. Some books concentrate on single makers – Ysart, for example – while others focus on important collections of paperweights, such as those in the Bergstrom-Mahler Museum, Wisconsin.

The annual bulletins of the Paperweight Collectors' Association will keep you abreast of the latest developments and recent research. Back numbers contain much authoritative reference. Auction catalogs and price lists are also useful, and the promotional leaflets of the glassmakers themselves contain interesting information.

F A C T O R Y   V I S I T S

Factory visits are an enjoyable way of discovering some of the secrets of the glassmakers' craft. Until comparatively recently, glassmaking was a fairly secretive business, and even today some factories are unwilling to admit visitors. Most, however, now recognize the commercial value of allowing visitors in.

The Scottish factories Caithness Glass, in Perth, Perthshire Paperweights, in Crieff, and Selkirk Glass, in Selkirk, all have special visitor centers with well-organized viewing facilities.

The prevalence of studio artists in the United States does not lend itself so easily to organized viewing, but there is a fairly open attitude, and some artists, including Paul Stankard and Victor Trabucco, have produced videos of their activities.

E X H I B I T I O N S

A keen collector will always appreciate the opportunity to see fine examples of the paperweight art. Such opportunities occur from time to time when quality collections are offered at auction, but special paperweight exhibitions generally provide a more comprehensive coverage, and are often backed by expert literature and commentary.

Temporary exhibitions organized by local societies are well worth visiting, but by their nature they cannot match the quality of the permanent exhibitions in a number of museums. The most outstanding exhibition to date was staged in 1978 by the Corning Museum of Glass, New York, when some 300 of the very finest paperweights in the world were assembled. This exhibition was recorded in the book *Paperweights: Flowers which Clothe the Meadows*, now regarded as an important work of reference.

For many years the United States has been the dominant area of paperweight activity, and it is not surprising that there has been a consistent one-way flow of 19th-century products from Europe. Most of the finest weights ever made are now in U.S. museums or private collections. The most important U.S. collections on public display are listed on page 79.

C O L L E C T O R   S O C I E T I E S

Membership of a collector society is essential for all serious collectors. A well-established group will organize meetings that will offer opportunities to meet other collectors, to buy and sell,

A B O V E
This superb bouquet from Baccarat includes some particularly fine flowers. Baccarat made three kinds of pansy, and this is one of the less common types. The red rose is known as a thousand-petal rose; it is highly valued as an individual flower, especially when it is this rich red. The white double clematis with honeycomb center that completes the trio is a striking contrast to the other two flowers.

RIGHT
This magnificent millefiori pedestal was made by Perthshire Paperweights in 1990. The canes in the mushroom-shaped head are very complex and of extremely fine quality. The pillar contains vertically placed white filigree canes, which fold under the mushroom head. Examination reveals that it was made in three sections – the head, the pillar, and the base.

ABOVE
This orchid is a good example of the bold, broad-petalled style of Lundberg Studios. It was made using torchwork techniques in 1984.

and to hear expert speakers. It may also hold special events such as identification sessions, organize two- or three-day conventions, and run field visits to factories or museums. Some societies produce newsletters to keep members in touch with national and international events, new artists, recent publications, and other developments. Membership of a society is also a useful way of establishing contact with dealers.

Some societies are run by a maker or dealer, and their primary objective is to promote sales. As long as this is borne in mind, they can be useful, although their range of activities will be more limited than those of non-commercial organizations, which will also provide more objectivity to their members in terms of assessment of literature and so forth.

ACQUIRING PAPERWEIGHTS

Your first paperweight will probably have been acquired by chance. It may have been an impulse buy, and may have been followed by similar purchases from the same source. Then, having succumbed to the collecting bug, you will wish to acquire others, but have no idea of alternative sources. Collecting paperweights, although growing in popularity, in no way compares with the other areas of collecting such as postage stamps or porcelain and silver. In fact, in most large towns you will be hard pressed to find a single outlet dealing in collector quality weights, and even in the high-class crystal and china stores you will usually find only basic gift types and those at the lower end of the collector range.

Before you turn to a dealer or auction house, however, there are one or two points to consider. The size of your budget is the most important factor. This will determine both the size and scope of your collection, and whether you will confine yourself to modern weights or go for the antiques. You should also decide if you want to specialize on a particular sector, or if you are going to build a wide-ranging collection. Whatever your budget and whatever the focus of your collection, do not hurry. The emphasis must always be on quality before quantity, and remember that you will make the biggest mistakes in the early stages of your collection.

DEALERS

A specialized dealer will probably be your first port of call, and will provide the best all-round source for modern weights and, probably, for antiques. As well as engaging in the customary buying and selling, paperweight dealers have a good record in providing a range of other support services for collectors. Those services are partly promotional, but most dealers have a genuine love of paperweights, quite apart from their commercial interest, and some are collectors themselves.

There is a wide range in the type of dealer and in the scope of what they have to offer. At the top end are those in the United States, some of whom have made a substantial contribution to the paperweight business through the production of books and product catalogs, the promotion of new artists, the provision of newsletters, and support for collector societies. Addresses of some notable dealers are given on page 79. In addition, the Annual Bulletin of the P.C.A. provides a comprehensive list, with some dealers in Austria, Canada, Germany, Switzerland, and Great Britain. Specialized dealers in Britain are harder to find, but some of the main ones are listed on page 79. For collectors who are unable to attend auctions or are shy of doing so, dealers are often prepared to bid on behalf of their clients, although they will, of course, charge a small fee for the service rendered.

MANUFACTURERS

Manufacturers sometimes sell direct to collectors. All three of the main Scottish factories have visitor centers with retail shops attached, which offer the advantage of a wide choice of current production. The French factory Baccarat will sell direct from Paris to overseas customers.

Addresses of some notable dealers are given on page 79.

BELOW

A lovely, three-dimensional dark red rose made by Baccarat in 1976. The petals are shaded to emphasize the relief, and little dew drop bubbles have been set among the petals. Although the latticinio is rather loose, it provides a pleasing background.

ABOVE

The attractive combination of pink on green jasper was used a few times by St. Louis in the 19th century. Baccarat repeated the formula in 1985 with two unusual stylized roses. The roses are flat, but they have been set sufficiently above the green jasper ground to cast their shadows on it, creating a spatial effect. The jasper ground is extremely well done, appearing as bright green moss. The ladybug on the foliage has been used many times in recent years by Baccarat and other makers.

ANTIQUE SHOPS

Antique shops and fairs ought to be a fruitful source for the 19th-century weights, but in fact they seldom are, and those seeking to build a collection through this route will be disappointed. It is every collector's dream to find a Baccarat butterfly on a flower lurking in some forgotten corner, but you are more likely to find the occasional green glass dump or a 20th-century product, typically from Murano. Some of the better class antique dealers may have the genuine article, but they will be very rare, and their prices are likely to be on the high side.

This will, therefore, not be a primary source to build the substance of the collection – but keep looking, because it is part of the fun of the chase, and one day you might be lucky.

AUCTIONS

Buying at auction is a good option for those deciding to collect antiques, but there are some potential hazards. Most weights sold from the major auction houses are to dealers. In theory, the collector can obtain antiques at dealer-cost, thereby saving some 30 percent, but in fact it does not work like that. To bid at auction, you have to know your values. Prices can change very dramatically from one auction to another, depending on who is in the room or on the phone. It only needs two collectors intent on getting the same lot to produce a crazy price. The presence of international dealers is another important factor. In London, for example, a small sale is unlikely to attract international interest and the prices should be reasonable, but a sale with more than 80 paperweight lots and including several really good ones will attract buyers from the United States, France, Germany, and Austria. It is, therefore, not unusual to find some prices at auction higher than those charged by a local dealer who has other sources of supply. Do not buy at auction until you have attended a few to gain experience of how they work, and until you have a reasonable knowledge of correct values for the types you intend to bid for.

Once you have reached that stage, however, you will find the auction room very exciting. However, a disciplined approach is called for. The most important part of an auction is the viewing, which should ideally be done a few days before the sale. Examine each weight in which you are interested very carefully, checking for flaws, damage, and the extent of restoration, which nearly all lots will have received. It all seems obvious, but some things

ABOVE
This attractive chequer was made by Perthshire Paperweights in 1992. It is similar to the Baccarat chequer dated 1849 in the Morton D. Barker Collection in the Illinois State Museum, U.S.A.

ABOVE
This Tudor rose was made by Perthshire in 1975. Its retail price in the U.K. was $70. At auction in the U.S.A. in 1993 an example sold for $358.

BELOW
In 1993 a 1979 Whitefriars concentric weight, with central silhouette bird, sold at auction in the U.S.A. for $495. This example, with a similar cane arrangement, the same cutting style, but with a butterfly silhouette, was also made in 1979.

ABOVE
Millefiori weights of this pattern were standard production items of the Strathearn factory in Scotland in the 1960s and 1970s. In 1993 they are offered by dealers at prices in the region of $85.

easily escape notice, and even seasoned experts have been known to miss an internal crack, the most serious of all types of damage.

After the viewing, take time to check what has been paid for similar types at previous auctions, and decide just how much you are prepared to pay. On the day, you must have a bidding strategy worked out. You may be interested in five lots but can afford to buy only one. Unfortunately, the one you like best is the fourth to come up, but you are determined to get one because the next auction is six months away. This is where you must carefully fix the maximum you will pay for each in turn. Having fixed the price, you must stick to it and not get carried away in the atmosphere of the auction room. If things go well, you get that fourth item.

Auctions of paperweights take place in several centers, but Santa Cruz (L. H. Selman), New York (Sotheby's), London (Christie's, Sotheby's, and Phillips), and Paris (Boisgirard) are the main ones. The quantity of 19th-century weights coming to auction has diminished over the years, and they are now rarely sufficient to justify a sale on their own. The main auction houses are concerned primarily with antique fine art, and rarely deal with modern paperweights, which usually appear with other glass and porcelain. L. H. Selman holds two "absentee" auctions a year, circulating to clients a catalog with every lot illustrated in color, and covering 19th- and 20th-century items over the complete price range.

Visiting the major auctions and buying the Selman catalogs will allow the keen collector to keep up to date with what is happening in the open market.

VALUE

By now you will have realized that collecting glass paperweights is not exactly a cheap hobby, although it does not necessarily have to be prohibitively expensive. The price of a weight will depend on when, where, and how it was purchased. Values change with time, vary according to country of purchase, and with the type of selling agent – manufacturer, dealer, or auctioneer.

Modern weights purchased new represent the safest option for early acquisitions. The established factories publish annual price lists, and the new products will be in mint condition, and, in general, there will be a more consistent relationship between intrinsic merit and selling price.

The lowest price will usually be in the country of origin, largely

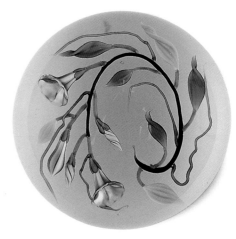

because of shipping and distribution costs. Buying at the factory shop will be a low-cost option, but will not necessarily be lower than from dealers in the same country, as manufacturers will not adopt a policy that would antagonize their principal selling channels.

Used modern weights normally take many years to appreciate in value. They can often be purchased from a dealer at a lower than original cost, and a collector wishing to sell must recognize this. The gross profit on luxury consumer durables will be within 35 or 50 percent of the selling price. A dealer seeking to add to his/her stock of older weights will, therefore, seek to buy at a price that will enable the normal profit percentage to be obtained. This means that a collector selling a modern weight, many years after the original purchase, will probably be incurring a loss on the deal.

For the novice collector, antique weights are the most difficult and potentially dangerous to acquire because prices often have little to do with the intrinsic merit of the article, and can vary widely. Because of the high values attributed on the grounds of rarity, it is better to begin to build an antique collection with good examples of the more basic types. A good Clichy millefiori of scattered canes in clear glass might be obtained for around

RIGHT

This superb bouquet of pink peace roses is the work of Rick Ayotte, one of the foremost U.S. studio artists. His weights are outstanding for their realism as well as for their appearance. Some, such as this one, come in almost magnum size. Costing $900 in 1992, this one represents good value.

BELOW

The Baccarat close millefiori with a *B1848* date-cane is a standard type that is frequently seen at auction. It is, nevertheless, much in demand as a fine example of 19th-century millefiori, and examples seldom fail to secure a good price. This one sold for $1,600 in London in 1992.

RIGHT

This St. Louis fruit on a basket of latticinio is another type that is frequently encountered. It represents good value for those in the early stages of building an antique collection – it cost $1,000 in 1991.

ABOVE

This rather disorganized type of paperweight is called a scrambled or end-of-day weight. The Clichy versions such as this, which was made *c.*1850, are very colorful and well regarded by collectors. This one cost $530 at a London auction in 1993.

$650–$700, and a Baccarat miniature lampwork pansy, the most often seen of all floral weights, for perhaps $600.

When moving up the scale, it is as well to know some of the explanations for premium prices for seemingly basic types. A date-cane, for example, will always add to the price for Baccarat and St. Louis millefiori weights, and could add more than $1,500 for a Venetian weight. A *C* signature-cane in a Clichy weight will also add considerably to the price.

Rose canes probably appear in more than half of Clichy millefiori weights, and individually carry no premium; collectively in a garland, however, they will be more highly valued. The rose coloring is usually pink and white. Other colors will have an added interest, and may add a nominal increment; a yellow one will add $300–$450. Clichy flowers are uncommon, and in lampworked form are much higher priced than Baccarat or St. Louis. The prices of Baccarat flowers will bewilder the newcomer, as in fact they often do for mature collectors.

Over recent years, the values of antique weights have held fairly firm, even through recessionary periods, but they have not made significant gains above the rate of inflation. The inevitable conclusion is that one would be ill-advised to take up collecting with a primary view to investment, either in modern or antique weights. The motivation should be love of the objects, and the pleasure they give in both the search and the ownership.

LOOKING AFTER YOUR COLLECTION

Glass is a fragile commodity, but the solid paperweight is surprisingly durable. Nevertheless, it needs careful handling, as the condition of many of the antiques will attest.

······················ C O N D I T I O N ·····················

The first principle of care is to make sure that the weight is in good shape before you buy it. Modern weights should be in pristine condition, but you may be more tolerant of antiques. Some will appear in prime condition, and these are likely to have been restored as described on page 64. Others will have surface scratches, chips, or bruises. The worst form of damage is the internal crack; never accept a weight damaged in this way for it could split at any time. How far other damage is acceptable is a matter of judgement, and the acid test is whether you are prepared to live with it. Sometimes a weight may appear to be so scarred that the motif is almost obscured by scratches. If they are not deep, restoration may work wonders. But you must go to an experienced restorer, who will not only see that the original profile is maintained, but will not leave tell-tale lumps and depressions.

Most antiques have already been restored, and the extent and quality of the work must be assessed. If too much glass has been removed from the original, it may have altogether spoiled it. Only you can judge whether this is the case. Residual lumps and depressions can have a disastrous effect on the visual quality. If a weight does not look quite right, close your eyes and rotate it in one hand, while feeling lightly with the fingertips of the other.

······························· C A R E ······························

Keep your paperweights away from direct sunlight, which can cause the glass to expand and break. In addition, if it is exposed to sunlight for long periods, clear glass can become clouded and assume a grey appearance. Water or damp is bad for glass, because the chemicals in the moisture can stain it.

Although glass is subject to extremely high temperatures in the making, it cannot withstand rapid changes. Never wash glass under warm running water. The glass is likely to shatter long before your hands feel the heat. If you have to wash them, do it in lukewarm soapy water.

ABOVE

William Manson has produced a number of weights incorporating aventurine, which has been particularly effective for marine subjects. This colorful environmental scene features a fire lizard made using aventurine. It is interesting to note that in 1984, when this weight was made, U.S. studio artists were also beginning to introduce environmental landscapes!

ABOVE

This paperweight case would be suitable for dealers, or for collectors with ambitious objectives at auction. The case is standard, and the insert is custom-cut from latex foam with a soft baize covering. The insert is easily taken out, and it is advisable to specify more than one configuration of recesses to allow for different combinations of paperweight sizes. It was supplied by a specialized case company, whose main customers are commercial organizations requiring custom-built sales kits.

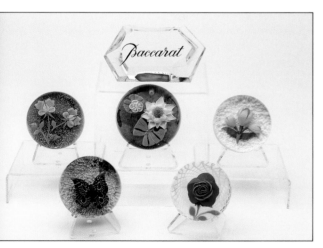

ABOVE

This little arrangement shows how stands and bridges can be used to create a pleasant display by making the best use of limited space.

··· DISPLAYING YOUR COLLECTION ···

Display becomes an issue when your collection has grown to a fair size, and when it is important to set them out well.

Paperweights are usually housed in a display cabinet, but unless it has been custom-designed for the purpose, it is unlikely to be satisfactory. Paperweights need to be well illuminated, which means that a cabinet should have large, clear glass windows, glass sides and shelves, and a non-reflective white background. If the cabinet has internal lighting, it should be of modern high-lumen/low-wattage lamps to avoid the high temperature caused by conventional illumination in confined spaces.

Most important of all is the density of display in relation to the area of the glass shelf. Glass becomes more fragile with age, and there is a limit to how much weight a shelf can stand. Paperweights are extremely heavy in aggregate, and accidents arising from this are not unknown. Ideally, the shelf should be about 5 inches deep and ¼ inch thick; there should be a span between supports of not more than 18 inches. If the shelves do not conform to this specification, great care must be exercised in the arrangement, so that the number of weights on each shelf is kept within bounds. The heavier ones should be placed near the supports. If the area of glass is greatly in excess of the stated measurements, it will be necessary to display your weights among other lighter objects, such as porcelain, so that the whole display does not seem too sparse.

Keen collectors often have custom-built fixtures in their homes. Plastic display stands of varying sizes can be obtained from good dealers, and these tilt the weights forward so that they are seen from the best angle. Display tables are effective, and do not require stands. However, the best way to display your collection is to show it in the open. In this way lighting ceases to become a problem, and you have much greater flexibility in arranging a large number into small spaces. The best arrangements will use plastic bridges, which are standard items of equipment for shops.

As your collection grows, you may wish to group the products of the various makers together, and to label them. Some manufacturers produce stands or nameplates for the purpose, or you may have to prevail upon some kind dealer to let you have the crystal nameplates intended as point-of-sale promotional equipment.

GLOSSARY

Air ring An elongated circular bubble, usually found next to a torsade.

Arrowhead cane A millefiori cane with a three-pronged arrowhead motif.

Basal rim The circular rim around a concave base where the weight is worn by contact with the surface on which it is placed.

Batch The word for the ingredients used to make the glass.

Block A wooden block with a concave interior used by craftsmen to shape the dome of the weight.

Bouquet de mariage A millefiori mushroom with a head composed entirely of white stardust canes.

Cog cane A millefiori cane with a cogged edge.

Collar The metal ring placed around the jig holding assembled canes so that they can be picked up on a gather of molten glass.

Crimp A metal tool with plates fashioned in a floral shape that is used to push colored glass into clear molten glass to shape the motif.

Crimped cane A corrugated cane.

Cullet Broken glass added to the batch.

Diamond cut V-shaped grooves cut into the base of the weight in a crisscross pattern; also called hobnail cut or strawberry cut.

Double overlay A weight that has been coated with one color over white to produce an opaque casing into which facets are cut to form windows (printies or punties).

Eidelweiss cane A white, star-shaped cane with a center made of tiny yellow rods, used extensively by Clichy in the 19th century.

Flash A coating of transparent colored glass, usually applied to the base of a weight. The technique was often used by St. Louis in the 19th century with amber-colored glass. A flash overlay is a single coating of colored glass over the whole weight.

Footed weight A weight with a flange at the base. This is not the same as a piédouche or pedestal weight, which has a pillar or stem like a mushroom.

Fortress cane A cane with a cross section resembling a small castle, with a square central keep and four corner towers. This cane was peculiar to Baccarat in the 19th century and was often used in conjunction with arrowhead canes.

Gather A portion of molten glass gathered from the furnace on the end of a pontil rod.

Hand-cooler An egg-shaped glass fashion accessory for ladies.

Hobnail cut See diamond cut.

Honeycomb cane A cane with a cross section resembling a honeycomb, but the cells are not necessarily hexagonal. In the 19th century, Baccarat produced some with star-shaped and some with circular cells; the Islington Glass Works produced rectangular ones.

Intaglio A motif set flush into the ground.

Macédoine The French word for hodgepodge, used to describe a scrambled or end-of-day weight.

Magnum A large weight with a diameter of more than 3¼ inches.

Marver The flat surface on which a gather of molten glass on the end of a pontil rod is rolled. Today the surface is usually made of iron; in the 19th century, it was of marble.

Metal The term used in the industry for glass, especially when molten.

Miniature A small weight with a diameter of not more than 2 inches.

Match-head cane A solid, opaque rod, usually yellow, used in the center of a flower and having the appearance of a match-head. The cane was a specialty of the St. Louis factory in the 19th century.

Moss cane A cane made of many white rods coated with green. A specialty of the Clichy factory.

Overlay A weight that has been coated with colored glass into which facets are cut to form windows (printies or punties).

Pastry mold A cane that looks like a lady's skirt viewed from above and flaring out towards the base. The center is filled with millefiori rods, etc. Pastry molds were the most often used Clichy canes.

Pontil rod The steel rod used by glassmakers to dip into the furnace to extract a gather of glass.

Profile The outline shape of a weight viewed from its side.

Printy A U.K. term for punty.

Punty A facet cut on the surface of a weight using a grinding wheel.

Star-cut A multi-pointed star cut into the base of a weight to enhance its appearance.

Stardust cane A cane consisting of several opaque white stars.

Strawberry cut See diamond cut.

Striations or striae Streaks in the glass caused by working with material of inconsistent density and giving a "heatwave" effect when viewed from the side.

Triple overlay A weight coated with a color over white over a color, so that both the exterior and the interior of the overlay are colored. In a double overlay the interior is nearly always white. These were produced rarely by the St. Louis factory in the 19th century.

Whorl A cane that has the appearance of the cross section of a jelly roll. It can be open-ended or be a series of concentric rings. When it is formed of red and white concentric rings, it is sometimes called a bull's-eye cane.

PAPERWEIGHT MAKERS

Belgium	Val St. Lambert	*Various*
	Verrerie Bougard	*Miscellaneous*
	Verrerie Nationale	*Miscellaneous*
Bohemia		*Millefiori*
France	Baccarat	*Various*
	Clichy	*Various*
	Pantin	*Lampwork*
	St. Louis	*Various*
	St. Mandé	*Millefiori*
Italy	P. Bigaglia	*Millefiori*
	G. B. Franchini	*Millefiori*
U.K.	Apsley Pellatt	*Sulfides*
	John Ford	*Sulfides*
	Bacchus	*Millefiori*
	Islington Glass Works	*Millefiori*
	Kilner	*Dumps*
	Whitefriars	*Millefiori*
U.S.A.	Boston & Sandwich Glass Co.	*Various*
	Dorflinger Glass Works	*Lampwork*
	Gillinder & Sons	*Millefiori*
	Mount Washington Glass Co.	*Lampwork*
	New England Glass Co.	*Various*

China		*Various*
France	Baccarat	*Various*
	D'Albret	*Sulfides*
	St. Louis	*Various*
Italy	Murano	*Various*
Malta	Mdina	*Abstract*
New Zealand	Peter Raos	*Floral*
Sweden	Kosta	*Abstract*
	Orrefors	*Abstract*
U.K.	Caithness Glass	*Various*
	John Deacons	*Various*
	Hartley Wood	*Dumps*
	Langham Glass	*Abstract*
	Liskeard	*Abstract*
	William Manson	*Lampwork*
	Monart/Vasart	*Millefiori*
	Okra	*Abstract*
	Perthshire Paperweights	*Various*
	Michael Rayner	*Abstract*
	Selkirk Glass	*Various*
	Strathearn	*Various*
	William Walker	*Abstract*
	Whitefriars	*Millefiori*
	Paul Ysart	*Various*
U.S.A.	Rick Ayotte	*Lampwork*
	Ray, Bob, and Bobbie Banford	*Lampwork*
	Chris Buzzini	*Lampwork*
	Cape Cod Glass	*Millefiori*
	John Choko and Pete Lewis	*Lampwork*
	Correia Art Glass	*Various*
	Jim Donofrio	*Lampwork*
	Drew Ebelhare	*Millefiori*
	Andrew Fote	*Surface patterned*
	Randall Grubb	*Lampwork*
	Harold Hacker	*Lampwork*
	Ronald Hansen	*Lampwork*
	Charles Kaziun	*Various*

Kontes Brothers	*Lampwork*
Charles and David Lotton	*Lampwork*
Dominic Labino	*Lampwork*
Lundberg Studios	*Various*
Michael O'Keefe	*Abstract*
Orient & Flume	*Various*
Parabelle Glass	*Millefiori*
Ken Rosenfeld	*Lampwork*
David Salazar	*Lampwork*
Barry Sautner	*Cameo & Diatetra (undercutting)*
James Shaw	*Abstract*
Gordon Smith	*Lampwork*
Paul Stankard	*Lampwork*
Delmo and Debbie Tarsitano	*Lampwork*
George Thiewes	*Surface patterned*
Victor, Jon, and David Trabucco	*Lampwork*
Mayauel Ward	*Lampwork*
Whitall Tatum Co.	*Lampwork*
Francis Whittemore	*Lampwork*

FURTHER READING

Bedford, John, *Collectors' Pieces: Paperweights*, New York, 1968

Bergstrom, Evangeline H., *Old Glass Paperweights*, Chicago, 1940; London, 1947

Casper, Geraldine J., *Glass Paperweights of the Bergstrom-Mahler Museum*, United States Historical Press, 1989

Casper, Geraldine, J. *Glass Paperweights*, Art Institute of Chicago, 1991

Cloak, Evelyn Campbell, *Glass Paperweights of the Bergstrom Art Center*, Crown Publishers, New York and London, 1969

Drysdale, Stuart, *Art of the Paperweight: Perthshire*, Paperweight Press, CA, 1983

Elville, E. M., *Paperweights and Other Glass Curiosities*, Country Life Ltd., 1954

Flemming, Monika and Pommerencke Peter, *Paperweights: Gläserne Briefbeschwerer*, Farfalla, Germany, 1993

Green, Charlotte, *Presse Papiers de Cristal*, 1990

Hollister, Paul, *The Encyclopedia of Glass Paperweights*, London, 1969

Hollister, Paul, *Glass Paperweights at Old Stourbridge* (The Cheney Wells Collection), 1969

Hollister, Paul, *Glass Paperweights of the New York Historical Society*, Clarkson N. Potter Inc., New York, 1974

Hollister, Paul, *Glass Paperweights: An Old Craft Revived*, 1975

Hollister, Paul and Lanmon, Dwight P., *Paperweights: Flowers which Clothe the Meadows*, The Corning Museum of Glass, 1978

Imbert, R. and Amic, *Les Presse Papiers Français*, Art et Industrie, Paris, 1948

Ingold, Gerard, *Art of the Paperweight: St. Louis*, Paperweight Press, Santa Cruz, CA, 1981

Jargstorf, Sibylle, *Paperweights*, Schiffer Publishing, PA, 1992

Johnson, Glen S., *The Caithness Collection*, 1981

Jokelson, Paul, *Antique French Paperweights*, privately published, 1955

Jokelson, Paul, *One Hundred of the Most Important Paperweights*, privately published, 1966

Jokelson, Paul, *Sulfides: The Art of Cameo Encrustation*, Thomas Nelson & Sons, New York, 1968

Jokelson, Paul and Tarshis, Dena, *Cameo Encrustation: The Great Sulfide Show*, Paperweight Press, CA, 1988

Jokelson, Paul and Ingold, Gerard, *Paperweights of the 19th and 20th Centuries*, Papier Presse, Phoenix, 1990

Kovacek, Michael, *Paperweights*, 1987

Kulles, George N., *Identifying Antique Paperweights*, Paperweight Press, CA, 1985

Kulles, George N., *Identifying Antique Paperweights: Lampwork*, Paperweight Press, CA, 1987

McCawley, Patricia K., *Antique Glass Paperweights from France*, Spink & Son Ltd., London, 1968

McCawley, Patricia K., *Glass Paperweights*, Charles Letts & Co Ltd., London, 1975

Mackay, James, *Glass Paperweights*, Ward Lock Ltd., 1973

Manheim, Frank, *A Garland of Weights*, Farrar, Strauss & Gironx, New York, 1967

Mannoni, Edith, *Sulfures et Boules Presse Papiers*, Editions Ch. Massin, Paris, 1972

Mannoni, Edith, *Classic French Paperweights*, Paperweight Press, CA, 1984 (English translation from the 1972 French edition, edited by Paul Jokelson and L. H. Selman)

Melvin, Jean S., *American Glass Paperweights and their Makers*, Thomas Nelson & Sons, New York, 1967

Newell, Clarence, *Old Glass Paperweights of Southern New Jersey*, Papier Presse, Phoenix, 1989

Penwell, Ellen, *The Morton D. Barker Paperweight Collection*, Illinois State Museum, 1985

Redus Gayle, Mary, *Glass Paperweights from the Estelle Doheny Collection*, 1971

Rossi, Sara, *Letts Guide to Collecting Paperweights*, Charles Letts & Co Ltd., London, 1990

Sarpellon, Giovanni, *Miniature di Vetro: Murrine 1838–1924*, Arsenale Editrice, Venice, 1992

Selman, Lawrence H., *Paperweights for Collectors*, Paperweight Press, CA, 1975

Selman, Lawrence H., *The Art of the Paperweight*, Paperweight Press, CA, 1988

Selman, Lawrence H., *All About Paperweights*, Paperweight Press, CA, 1991

Spink & Son Ltd., *Flora in Glass* (Paul Stankard Exhibition), 1981

Turner, Ian, Clark, Alison and Andrews, Frank, *Ysart Glass*, Volo Edition Ltd., London, 1990

Wheaton Museum of Glass, *American Glass Paperweights*, Wheaton Historical Association, 1939

Wheaton Museum of Glass, *Paul Joseph Stankard: The First Decade*, Wheaton Historical Assocation, 1979

Paperweight Collectors' Association, Annual Bulletins from 1954

USEFUL ADDRESSES

COMMERCIAL SOCIETIES
International Paperweight Society
L. H. Selman
761 Chestnut Street
Santa Cruz, California 95060
Tel: (408) 427-1177

Caithness Collectors Club
Caithness Glass plc.
Inveralmond, Perth
Scotland PH1 3TZ
Tel: (0738) 37373
There are local groups in Australia,
Canada, Germany, Netherlands,
Switzerland, and the United States.

NON-COMMERCIAL SOCIETIES
Paperweight Collectors Association
8 Carol Avenue
Easthampton, Massachusetts 01027
Tel: (413) 527-2598

Michel-Pierre Grenier
3275 Sherbrook Street East #2
Montreal, Quebec H1W 1CS
Canada
Tel: (514) 523-9580

Phyllis Helfand
16 Tanburn Place
Don Mills, Ontario M3A 1X5
Canada
Tel: (416) 447-4659

Peter Pommerencke
Postfach 1233
D-8033 Planegg
Germany

John Miles
42 Motueka Street
Nelson
New Zealand
Tel: (03) 548-2362

Cambridge Paperweight Circle
34 Huxley Road
Welling, Kent
UK
Tel: (081) 303-4663

COLLECTIONS TO VISIT
The most important collections on public
display in the United States are:
The Art Institute of Chicago
Michigan Avenue at Adams Street
Chicago, Illinois 60603
Tel: (312) 443-3600

The Bergstrom-Mahler Glass Museum
165 North Park Avenue
Neenah, Wisconsin 54956
Tel: (414) 722-3348

The Corning Museum of Glass
Corning Glass Center
Corning, New York 14831
Tel: (607) 937-5371

Illinois State Museum
Springfield, Illinois 62706
Tel: (217) 782-7152

Strong Museum
Manhatten Square
Rochester, New York 14607
Tel: (716) 263-2700

Wheaton Museum of American Glass
Millville, New Jersey 08332
Tel: (609) 825-6800

There is a permanent exhibition of
mainly 20th-century weights at:

Yelverton Paperweight Centre
Leg o' Mutton
Yelverton, Devon PL20 6AD, U.K.
Tel: (0822) 854250

DEALERS

UNITED STATES
Paul and Karen Dunlop
P.O. Box 82370
Phoenix, Arizona 85071–2370

Leo Kaplan
967 Madison Avenue
New York, New York 10021

L. H. Selman
761 Chestnut Street
Santa Cruz, California 95060

UNITED KINGDOM
Garrick Coleman
5 Kensington Court
London W8 5DL

Delamosne & Son Ltd.
Court Close
North Raxall, Chippenham
Wiltshire SN14 7AD (antiques only)

Mallett & Son
141 New Bond Street
London W1Y 0BS (antiques only)

Sweetbriar House
Robin Hood Lane
Helsby, Cheshire WA6 9NH

The Paperweight Collection
19 High Petergate
York YO1 2EN

The Stone Gallery
93 The High Street
Burford, Oxfordshire OX18 4QA

Yelverton Paperweight Centre
Leg o' Mutton
Yelverton, Devon PL20 6AD

INDEX

Numbers in *italics* refer to photographs.

Abstracts 17, 37–9, *37, 38, 39, 72, 77*

American weights 12, 13, 15, 16, 17, 29, 36, 38–9, 40, 42–3, 45, 50–2, 63–4, 67, 77

antique weights 8–9, 10–13, 24, 26, 27, 28, 29, 30–5, 40–4, 56–7, 58, 60, 69, 74
  buying 69–71, 72
  identifying 61–4

auctions 69, 70–1

aventurine 48, *48, 49,* 74

Ayotte, Rick *18,* 51–2, *51, 73,* 77

Baccarat *6, 7,* 12, *12, 14,* 15, 16, *16,* 24, *24,* 26, 27, 28, *29,* 30, *31,* 32–3, *33,* 34, 40, *40,* 41, 42, 43, 44, *44,* 45, 47, *47,* 49, 50, *56,* 57, 62, *62, 64, 67,* 69, *69,* 70, *72, 73, 73,* 77

Bacchus & Sons *11,* 34, *34,* 49, 63, 64, 77

Banford, Ray & Bob *46,* 50, *50,* 77

Belgian weights 12, 40, 70

Bigaglia, Pietro 11, 77

Bohemian weights *10,* 12, *14,* 15, 23, 29, 57, 62, 77

books 61, 65–6, 67, 78

Boston & Sandwich Glass Co. 42, 63, 77

bouquet weights *6,* 15, *16,* 22, 39, 41–2, *41, 43,* 45, 46, *46, 50,* 52, *52,* 65, *67, 73*

bubbles
  in abstracts 37–8, *37, 38, 72*
  in dumps 53, 54, *54*

Bussolin, Domenico 12

butterfly and flower weights 44, *44, 49*

buttons, glass 15, *23,* 50

Caithness Glass 17, *17,* 38, 39, *39,* 48, *49,* 67, 77

care of paperweights 74

carpet grounds 27, *27,* 33, *33,* 34

categories 21

chequers 26, *26,* 70

Chinese weights 17, 19–21, *19, 20, 72,* 77

Clichy 12, *12,* 23, *24,* 25, *25,* 26, *26,* 30–2, *31,* 33, 36, 41–2, *41,* 43, 57, *57,* 64, *65,* 72, 73, *73,* 77

Clichy rose *8,* 31, 57, 58, 73

color grounds *8,* 25, 27

Corning Museum of Glass 43, 67

Correia Art Glass *38,* 39, 77

Cristalleries de Pantin 12, *13,* 43, 77

crown weights *20,* 29–30, *30,* 57

cushion weights *21,* 49

Date-canes *26,* 32, 33, 34, 46, 49, 73, *73*

Deacons, John *30,* 48–9, *49, 57, 58,* 77

dealers 68, 69, 70, 72, 79

displaying paperweights 75, *75*

doorstops *see* dumps

Drysdale, Stuart 17, 49, 78

dumps 53–5, *53, 54, 55,* 77
  prices 55, 70

Dupont weights *14,* 15, *27, 32*

Early glassmaking 6

end-of-day weights *see* scrambled weights

English weights 12, 15, 34–6, 56, 77

engraving 52, *52, 59,* 60, *60*

environmental weights *47,* 52, *74*

Erlacher, Max 52, *52,* 60, *60*

exhibitions 67, 79

Faceting *12, 14,* 15, 37, 42, *43,* 49

filigree *10,* 23, 24, 26, 28, 29, 30, 34, 41, 49

floral weights *6, 9, 14,* 15, *15, 16, 18,* 20, *29, 30, 33,* 39, 40–1, *40, 41,* 42–3, *47,* 48, 49, 50, *50,* 51, *51,* 52, *52, 68,* 69, *72, 73*

flower pots 53, *53,* 54

fluorescence testing 64

Franchini, Giovanni 12, 31, 77

French weights 12, 15, 16, 23, 24, 25, 26, 29, 30–4, 35, 40–2, 43–4, 45, 46, 47, 49, 50, 56, 57, 58, 62, 63, 64, 69, 70, 72, 73, 77

fruit weights *18,* 43–4, *44, 46, 61, 73*

Garlands 26, *26, 27,* 31, *31,* 32, 41, 44, 73

gift weights 8, 17, 19–21, 36, 68

Gillinder weights *13,* 63–4, 77

Hollow weights 30, 36

Holmes, Peter 17, *17, 38,* 39

Iridescent glass 38–9, *55,* 59, *59*

Islington Glass Works 34, 77

Jasper grounds 29, *29,* 33, *69*

Jokelson, Paul 16, 17, 78

Kaziun, Charles 15, *15,* 16, 45, 50, 77

Lampwork *9,* 12, 13, *14, 15,* 16, 17, *18, 30,* 36, 37, 39–52, *40, 41, 43, 44, 45, 46, 47, 48, 49, 50, 51,* 52, *52, 72, 73,* 77
  antique 40–4
  with millefiori 41
  modern 45–52
  by studio artist 15, 16, 17, 45–6, 50–2, *73,* 77

latticinio 29, *30,* 41, *41,* 43, 49, 57, 73

limited editions 15, 17, 21, 33, 34, 39, 46

Lundberg Studios 38, 52, 59, *68,* 78

Manson, William 48, *49, 74,* 77

marbries 58–9, *58*

Mdina glass *37,* 77

millefiori:
  close *12, 16, 20, 22,* 23–4, *24,* 28, 31, 33, 34, 73
  concentric *8, 11, 12,* 25, *25,* 28, 31, 33, *34, 35, 71*
  history of 10–11
  with lampwork 41
  making 22–3
  scattered 25, 31, 33, *33, 72*
  with sulphides 57

modern weights 8, 13–18, 25, 27, 30, 33, 34, 35–9, 45–52, 57–8, 59, 62, 69, 74
  buying 71–2

Mount Washington Glass Co. 13, 42–3, *42, 66,* 77

Murano weights 17, 19–20, *20, 32, 63,* 70, 77

mushrooms *22,* 28, *28, 29,* 33, 34

New England Glass Co. 42, *43,* 77

O'Keefe, Michael 39, *39,* 77

Orient & Flume 38, 52, 58, 59, *59,* 77

overlay *21, 22, 29,* 47, 49, 76

Panel weights 28–9

Paperweight Collectors Association 16, 35, 66, 68, 78, 79

Parabelle Glass 36, *63,* 77

pedestal weights 29, *68*

Perthshire Paperweights *6,* 17, *17,* 21, *21, 27, 30,* 36, *36,* 45, 46, 48, 49, *49, 62,* 67, *68, 70,* 77

picture weights 20, 60, *60*

piédouche weights *see* pedestal weights

pinchbeck weights 60, *60*

plaques 13, 42–3, *42,* 55

prices 8, 39, 51, 54, 55, 58, 59, 60, 71–3

printies 47, 76

profiles 50, 64, *64,* 74, 76

punties *see* printies

Russian glass 13, 43

Sabellico 10

Saint (St) Louis 12, *12,* 16, *16, 22, 27,* 28, *28,* 29, *29,* 30, 33–4, *33,* 40, 41, *41,* 42, 43, *43,* 44, 45, 46, *46,* 49, *56,* 57, 58, *58,* 62, 63, *64, 73, 73,* 77

Scottish weights 15, 17, 21, 36, 39, 45, 46, 48–50, 58–9, 67, 69, 77

scrambled weights 30, *31, 73*

Selkirk Glass 17, *38,* 39, *56,* 58–9, *58, 62,* 67, 77

signature canes *26,* 32, 33, *46,* 48, 49, 63, 73

Silesia 11, 12

silhouettes *6, 10, 11, 13, 16, 17, 21,* 23, *27, 29,* 33, 34, 36, *71*

silver flower 54, *54*

snake weights 44

societies 16, 35, 66, 67–8, 79

sodden snow 25, *25,* 34

Stankard, Paul *9,* 17, *18, 45,* 50, 51, *51,* 52, *66,* 67, 77

Stourbridge weights 15, 34

Strathearn weights *23, 24, 71,* 77

studio artists 9, 15, 16, 45–6, 50–2, 67
  lampwork techniques 45–6
  sulphides 16, 54, *54,* 55–7, *56*

surface-patterned weights 59, *59,* 77

swirls 57–8, *57,* 58, *58*

Tarsitano, Delmo & Debbie *18,* 52, *52,* 61, 77

Terris, Colin 17, *17,* 39

Thiewes, George 59, *59,* 77

three-dimensional motifs *33, 47, 47,* 51–2, 69

torchwork 36, 52, *52,* 68

torsade 28, *28,* 29, *29,* 33, 34, 42, 43

Trabucco, Victor 52, *52,* 67, 77

Upset muslin 26, *26,* 27, 33

Venetian weights 11, 12, 48, 73 *see also* Murano weights

Whitall Tatum Co. 13, *14,* 50, 77

Whitefriars *8,* 15, 34–6, *34, 35, 36, 62, 71,* 77

Whittemore, Francis *16,* 47, 50, 77

window facets *see* printies

Ysart, Paul *9,* 15, *15,* 16, 45, 48, *48,* 49, 63, *63,* 64, 66, 77

ACKNOWLEDGEMENTS

Quintet Publishing would like to thank the following collectors, who kindly loaned their paperweights for photography: Mrs Anne Anderson, Roy Brown, Norman Faulkner, Owen Moore, Peter Pilbeam, Ted Ponting, Pat Reilly and Colin Silk. Thanks also to Jill Thomas-Clark at the Corning Museum of Glass, New York.